"Just What Do You Think You're Doing?"

She stared wordless̲̲̲ ̲̲̲̲̲̲ ̲̲̲̲̲̲ of the harsh angry voice, a vagu̲̲  moonlight.

"How did you get dislodging her cap form a fiery cascade down her back.

"What . . . the . . . You're a girl!"

"Sure, and that's observant of you—"

"From your accent, I could make a guess that you are little Dee, Paddy's niece."

"I am Adelia Cunnane, to be sure, but not your little Dee. And who might you be coming around to grab innocent people?"

"I'm Travis. *Travis Grant.*"

NORA ROBERTS

lives with her two sons in the Blue Ridge Mountains of western Maryland. To be a published author was her lifetime dream which she has seen fulfilled in the many books that she has written for Silhouette. Renowned for her warm characters and wit, Nora Roberts is a favorite with readers of romance.

Dear Reader:

In the three years since Silhouette Books began publishing with Silhouette Romances we've seen many new developments: American settings and heroines, stronger, more independent characters, longer, more sensual stories and some exciting new authors who have appeared on the scene.

It was during this first year that many of you discovered new favorites including Dixie Browning, Nora Roberts, Brooke Hastings and many others. These authors have continued to write new and exciting stories, whether they are for Silhouette Romance, Silhouette Special Edition, Silhouette Desire or for Silhouette Intimate Moments.

Don't miss this opportunity to buy all ten of your favorites from the "Springtime is Romance time" display wherever you buy books.

Karen Solem
Editor-in-Chief
Silhouette Books

NORA ROBERTS
Irish Thoroughbred

SILHOUETTE ROMANCE #81

Published by Silhouette Books New York
America's Publisher of Contemporary Romance

Silhouette Books by Nora Roberts

SILHOUETTE BOOKS, a Division of Simon & Schuster, Inc.
1230 Avenue of the Americas, New York, N.Y. 10020

ISBN: 0-671-50701-X

First Silhouette printing May, 1981

10 9 8 7 6 5

Chapter One

Adelia Cunnane stared out the window without seeing the magic layer of clouds. Some formed into mountains, others glaciers, flattening and thinning into an ice-encrusted lake; but, for one experiencing her first air journey, she found the view uninspiring. Her mind was crowded with doubts and uncertainties that merged with a strong pang of homesickness for a small farm in Ireland. But both farm and Ireland were now very far away, and every minute that crawled by brought her closer to America and strangers. She knew, with a sigh of frustration, that nothing in her life had ever prepared her properly to cope with either.

Her parents had been killed in a lorry accident, leaving her an orphan at the tender age of ten. In the weeks that followed her parents' death, Adelia had drifted through a fog of shock, turning inward to ward off the agony of separation, the strange and terrifying feeling of desertion. Slowly, a wall had been constructed around the pain, and she had thrown herself into the work of the farm with an adult's dedication.

Her father's sister, Lettie Cunnane, had taken over both child and farm, running both with a firm hand. Although never unkind, neither had she been affectionate: she had possessed little patience or understanding for the unpredictable, often tempestuous child.

The farm had been the only common ground between them, and woman and child had built their relationship with the dark, fertile soil and the hours of labor it required. They had lived and worked together for nearly thirteen years; then Lettie had suffered a paralyzing stroke, and Adelia had been forced to divide her time between the duties of the farm and caring for an invalid's needs. Days and nights had merged together as she waged the determined battle to shoulder the increasing responsibility.

Her enemies had been the lack of time and the lack of money. When, after six long months, she was again left alone, Adelia was near the point of exhausted desperation. Her aunt was gone, and though she had worked unceasingly, the farm had had to be sold for taxes.

She had written to her only remaining relative, her father's elder brother, Padrick, who had emigrated to America twenty years previously, informing him of his sister's death. His answer had been immediate, the letter warm and loving, asking her to join him. The last sentence of the missive was a simple, gentle command: "Come to America; your home is with me now."

So she had packed her few belongings, sold or given away what could not be taken with her, and said goodbye to Skibbereen and the only home she had ever known. . . .

A sudden movement of the plane jolted Adelia back from memory. She sat back against the cushions of her seat, fingering the small gold cross she always wore around her neck. There was nothing left for her in Ireland, she told herself, fighting against the flutters of her stomach. Everything she had loved there was dead, and Padrick Cunnane was the only family she had left, the only link with what she had once had. She pushed back a surge of sudden, unaccustomed fear. America, Ireland—what difference did it make? Her shoulders moved restlessly. She would manage. Hadn't she always managed? She was determined not to be a burden to her uncle, the vague, shadowy man she knew only from letters, whom she had last seen when barely three. There would be work for her, she reasoned, perhaps on the horse farm her uncle had written of so often over the years. Her ability to work with animals was innate, and she had absorbed a varied knowledge of medicine through her experiences, her skill being such that she had often been called on to aid in a difficult calving or stitch up a rent hide. She was strong, despite her diminutive stature—and, she reminded herself with an unconscious squaring of shoulders, she was a Cunnane.

Surely, she told herself with more confidence, there would be a place for her at Royal Meadows where her uncle worked as trainer for the Thoroughbred racing stock. There'd be no fields needing plowing, no cows needing milking, but she'd earn her bread and butter if she had to work as a scullery maid. She wondered suddenly, with a small frown, if they had scullery maids in America.

The plane touched down, and Adelia disembarked and entered the Dulles terminal in Virginia, where she found herself gaping in confusion, fascinated by the scene, confused by the babble of foreign tongues, the odd mixture of people. Her eyes lingered over an East Indian family in full native dress. She turned to observe two teenagers in faded denims strolling by hand in hand, followed by a scurrying middle-aged businessman clutching a leather briefcase.

Later, standing in the lobby, she looked around hoping to see a familiar face. Everyone rushing and hurrying, she thought. A body could be trampled and never seen again. . . .

"Dee, little Dee!" A man hurried toward her, a stockily built, compact man with a full thatch of curling gray hair, and she caught a glimpse of eyes as bright and blue as her father's before she was enveloped in a warm, crushing hug. The thought occurred to her that it had been a lifetime since anyone had held her so close.

"Little Dee, I would have known you anywhere." He pulled back and studied her face, eyes misty, smile tender. "It's like looking into Kate's face again—it's the image of your mother you are."

He continued to stare at her while she searched for her voice, his gaze taking in the deep, rich auburn hair falling in gleaming waves to her shoulders, the large, deep green of thickly lashed eyes, the tip-tilted nose and full mouth which Aunt Lettie had described as impudent, the face now of a startled pixie.

"What a beautiful sight you are," he said at last on a sigh of pure pleasure.

"Uncle Padrick?" she asked, finding a multitude of questions and emotions racing through her.

"And who else would you be thinking I might be?" He looked down at her with those well-remembered eyes, filled with love and laughter, and doubts, fears, and questions vanished in a wave of joy.

"Uncle Paddy," she whispered as she flung her arms around his neck.

As they drove along the highway from the airport, Adelia stared about her in fresh amazement. Never had she seen so many cars, and all flying by at an outrageous speed. Everything moved so fast, and the noise, she marveled silently, the noise was enough to wake the dead. Shaking her head, she began to bombard her uncle with questions.

How far was it they were going? Did everyone drive so fast in America? How many horses were at Royal Meadows? When could she see them? Questions buzzed in her mind and through her lips, and Paddy answered them tolerantly, finding the soft lilt of her voice as sweet as a summer breeze.

"Where is it I'll be working?"

He removed his eyes from the road a moment and glanced at her. "There's no need for you to be working, Dee."

"Oh, but Uncle Paddy, I must," she disagreed, turning to face him. "I could work with the horses; I've a way with animals."

Thick gray brows drew together in a doubtful frown. "I didn't bring you all this way to be putting you to work." Before she could protest, he went on. "And I don't know what Travis would be thinking about me hiring my own niece."

"Oh, but I'd do anything." She brushed back masses of chestnut hair. "Groom the horses, muck out the stalls, cart hay—it doesn't matter." Unknowingly, she used her eyes in an outrageous manner. "Please, Uncle Paddy, it's crazy I'd be in a week, not having some sort of work to do."

Her eyes won the small battle, and Paddy squeezed her hand. "We'll see."

So engrossed had she been in their conversation and the fascinating stream of traffic that she had lost all track of time. When Paddy pulled into a drive and halted the car, Adelia gazed about her with new wonder.

"Royal Meadows, Dee," he announced with a sweeping gesture of his hand. "Your new home."

The entrance to the long, winding drive was flanked by two tall stone pillars, and bushes studded with the promise of flowering buds continued along its path as far as she could see. The grass was brilliantly green over softly rolling hills, and horses grazed lazily in the distance.

"The finest horse farm in all of Maryland, sure as faith," Paddy added with possessive pride as he proceeded along the curving drive. "And—in Padrick Cunnane's opinion—the finest in the whole of America."

The car rounded a bend in the drive, and Adelia caught her breath as the main house came into view. An immense structure, or so it seemed to her, with three magnificent stories of old and muted stone. Dozens of windows winked in the gleaming sun like large, clear eyes. Wide and boldly glistening, they were a sharp contrast to the stone's mellowness. Skirting the top two stories were balconies, the design of wrought iron as intricate and delicate as the finest lace. The house stood on a gently sloping lawn of close-cropped green, graced with bushes and stately trees just awakening from their winter sleep.

"Beautiful, isn't it, Dee?"

"Aye," she agreed, awed by its size and elegance. "The grandest house I've ever seen."

"Well, our house isn't so grand as this." He turned the car left as the drive forked past the stone building. "But it's a fine place, and I hope you'll be happy there."

Adelia turned her attention to her uncle with a smile that transformed her face into a work of art. "I'll be happy, Uncle Paddy, as long as you're with me." Letting impulse guide her movements, she leaned over and kissed his cheek.

"Ah, Dee, I'm glad you're here." He took her hand in a firm grip. "You've brought the spring with you."

The car came to a halt, and Adelia turned to look

out the front window, her mouth falling open at what. greeted her eyes. An oval track commanded her view, and across from it stood a large white building, which Paddy identified as the stables. Fences and paddocks checkerboarded the area, and the scent of hay and horses drifted through the air.

In solemn amazement she gazed about, and the thought sped through her brain that she had not moved from one farm to another but from one world to another. At home, the farm had meant the earth, with its blessings and curses, a small barn in constant need of repair, a strip of pasture. Here, the space alone made her eyes widen, so much space to belong to one man. But as well as space, she recognized the efficiency and the order in fresh white buildings and split-rail fences. In the distance, where the hills began their soft roll, she saw mares grazing while their foals frolicked with the joy of spring and youth.

Travis Grant, she mused, recalling the name of the owner from Paddy's letters. *Travis Grant* knows how to care for what he owns. . . .

"There's my house." Now Paddy pointed out the opposite window. "Our house now."

Following his direction, she let out a cry of pleasure. The first story of the building was a large white garage, which she learned later serviced the trailers and trucks used for transporting the Thoroughbreds. Atop this was a stone structure, nearly twice as large as the farmhouse in which she had spent her life. It was a miniature replica of the main house, with the same native stonework and glistening windows graced with balconies.

"Come inside, Dee. Get a look at your new home."

He led her down a narrow, crushed stone path and up the stairs to the front door, opening it wide and nudging her ahead of him.

A bright, cozy room welcomed her, with pale green walls and a shining oak floor. A brightly checked sofa and matching chair invited her to sit in front of the raised hearth when the weather was cool, or contemplate rambling hills through wide, sheer-draped windows.

"Oh, Uncle Paddy!" She sighed, making an inadequate but expressive movement of her hands.

"Come, Dee, I'll show you the rest."

He led her through the house, her wide eyes growing larger with each new discovery, from the kitchen, with its sunny yellow fixtures and spotless counters, to the bath, where creamy ivory tiles made her dream of languishing for hours in hot, soapy water.

"This is your room, darlin'."

He opened the door across from the bath, and Adelia stepped inside. It was not an overly large room, but to her inexperienced eyes it was huge indeed. The walls were painted a robin's-egg blue, and sheer white curtains billowed and swayed at two opened windows. The soft blue and white was repeated in the flower print of the bedspread, and a fluffy white rug lay on the wooden floor. The mirror over the maple dresser reflected the expression of stunned pleasure on her face. The knowledge that the room was to be hers brought unaccustomed tears to her eyes. Blinking them away, she turned and threw her arms around her uncle's neck.

Later, they strolled across the lawn toward the stables. Adelia had changed from the dress she had worn for the trip and was now clad in her more customary attire of jeans and cotton shirt, with her auburn curls pulled up and covered by a faded blue hat. She had convinced her uncle that rest was not what she needed, and that seeing the horses was what she wanted above all else. With her face glowing and eyes pleading, Paddy would have found it impossible to deny her anything.

Approaching the stables, they spotted a small group gathered around a chestnut Thoroughbred. The raised voices reached uncle and niece before their presence was noted.

"And what might be the problem here?" Paddy demanded.

"Paddy, glad you're back," a tall, husky man greeted him with obvious relief. "Majesty just had one of his spells. Gave Tom a bad kick."

Paddy transferred his attention to a small, spare young man seated on the ground, nursing his thigh and muttering.

"How bad is it, lad? Did you break anything?"

"Naw, nothing broke." Disgust was more evident than pain in both voice and face. "But I don't guess I'll be riding for a couple of days." Looking over at the dark chestnut, he shook his head with a mixture of resentment and reluctant amusement. "That horse may be the fastest thing on four legs, but he's meaner than a stomped-on cat."

"His eyes aren't mean," Adelia commented, and several pairs of eyes focused on her for the first time.

"This is Adelia, my niece. Dee, this is Hank Manners, assistant trainer. Tom Buckley, on the ground there, is an exercise boy, and George Johnson and Stan Beall, grooms." After the introductions had been completed, Adelia quickly turned her attention back to the horse.

"They don't understand you, do they? Ah, but you're a fine fellow."

"Miss," Hank cautioned as she lifted a hand to stroke his muzzle, "I wouldn't do that. He's not in the best of moods to begin with, and he doesn't take to strangers."

"Ooch, but it's not strangers we'll be for long." Smiling, she stroked the length of his strong muzzle, and Majesty blew from wide nostrils.

"Paddy," Hank began in cautious warning, but the other man lifted a hand to silence him.

"A fine, beautiful horse you are. I've never seen another to compare with you, and that's the truth of it." She continued to speak as she ran her hands over his smooth neck and side. "You're built for running—strong, long legs and a fine, wide chest." Her hands moved over him freely as the horse remained still, ears at attention. She fondled his nose before resting her cheek against his neck. "I bet you're lonely for someone to talk to."

"I'll be switched." Hank observed Adelia's confident handling of the frisky colt and shook his head. "He's never let anyone do that before, not even you, Paddy."

"Animals have feelings as well, Mr. Manners."
She brought her face from the Thoroughbred's neck
and turned around. "He wants some pampering."

"Well, little lady, you certainly seem to have a
way with him." He gave her a grin expressive of both
amusement and admiration before turning his attention to Paddy. "He still needs to be exercised. I'll
give Steve a call."

"Uncle Paddy." Adelia grabbed his arm on impulse, eyes shining with excitement. "I can do it. Let
me take him out."

"I don't think a little lady like you could handle a
big fire-breather like Majesty," Hank put in before
Paddy could speak, and Adelia drew herself up to
the full of her five feet two inches and tilted her chin.

"There's nothing on four legs I can't ride."

"Is Travis back yet?" Paddy concealed his smile
and addressed Hank.

"No." He eyed Paddy through narrowed lids.
"You're not thinking of letting her take him out?"

"I'd say she's about the right size—couldn't weigh
over a hundred pounds." He gave his niece a
thorough survey, one hand rubbing his chin.

"Paddy." Hank's hand descended on his shoulder,
only to be ignored.

"You're a Cunnane, aren't you, lass? If you say
you can handle him, then by the saints you can."
Adelia beamed at her uncle and told him firmly
she was indeed a Cunnane.

"God knows what the boss is going to say when he
finds out," Hank muttered, finding himself against a
solid wall of family alliance.

"Just leave Travis to me," Paddy answered with calm authority.

With a shrug of his shoulders and another incoherent mutter, Hank resigned himself to Paddy's loss of common sense.

"Once around the track, Dee," her uncle instructed. "Pace him to what you can handle; I can see from the look of him he wants his head."

Pulling her cap lower, she nodded, watching the well-trimmed hooves paw the ground in impatience. With an easy vault she was in the saddle, and as Hank opened the wide gate she took Majesty onto the dirt track. Leaning forward, she whispered in his ear as he sidestepped and strained to be off.

"Ready, Dee?" Paddy called. As an afterthought he pulled out his stopwatch.

"Aye, we're ready." Straightening, she took a deep breath.

"Go!" he shouted, and horse and rider lunged down the track.

Crouching low over the Thoroughbred's neck, she urged him on to the speed for which he thirsted. The wind beat against her face, stinging her eyes, as they tore over the dirt at a pace she had never experienced, never imagined, but somehow had craved. It was a wild, exhilarating adventure; both horse and rider revelled in the unbridled sensation as they sped as one around the oval track, sun, wind, and speed their companions. She laughed and shouted to her partner, a new sense of freedom liberating her from the concerns and worries that had been a part of her life for so long. For a few short moments she was riding the clouds, away from pressure, away from responsibility, in a glorious haven that returned her to carefree childhood. When they came to the end of the run, she slowed the horse gradually to a halt and flung her arms around his gleaming neck.

"I'll be a son of a gun!" Hank said in simple astonishment.

"What were you expecting?" Paddy questioned, feeling as proud as a peacock with two tails. "She's a Cunnane." He held out the stopwatch for Hank to see. "Not a bad time either." With a final smile, he strutted over as Adelia slipped to the ground.

"Oh, Uncle Paddy!" Her eyes gleamed like emeralds against her flushed face, and she pulled off her cap, flourishing it in excitement. "He's the grandest horse in the world. It was like riding Pegasus himself!"

"That was nice riding, little lady." Hank extended his hand, shaking his head in admiration both for her ability and for the gleaming hair that now spilled over her shoulders.

"Thank you, Mr. Manners." She accepted his hand with a smile.

"Hank."

She grinned. "Hank."

"Well, Adelia Cunnane." Paddy slipped his arm around her shoulders. "Royal Meadows just hired another exercise boy. You've got yourself a job."

Lying in her bed that night, Adelia stared wide-eyed at the ceiling. So many things had happened, in so short a time, that her mind refused to relax and allow her body rest.

After her ride on the Thoroughbred, she had been taken through the stables, introduced to more hands and more horses, shown into a tackroom that contained more leather than she had ever seen in one place at one time, and exposed to more people and more things than she believed she had ever been exposed to in her life. And all in the course of one day.

Paddy had prepared their dinner, firmly refusing assistance, and she had merely watched as he bustled around the kitchen. The stove, she decided, had more to do with magic than technology. And a machine that washed and dried the dishes at a touch of a button—marvels! Hearing about such things and reading about them was one matter, but seeing them with your own eyes . . . it was easier to believe in the Pooka and the little people. When, with a sigh, she said as much to her uncle, he threw back his head and laughed until tears flowed down his cheeks, then enveloped her in a hug as crushing as the one he had greeted her with at the airport.

They had eaten in the small dinette set in the kitchen window, and she had answered all his questions about Skibbereen. The meal was full of talking and laughing, and Paddy's eyes twinkled continually at her colorful descriptions and outrageous stories. She elaborated here and there, her hands working with her words, brows raising over guileless eyes as she stretched truth into an obvious exaggeration. Her uncle had noticed the faint shadows under them, however, and urged her to retire early, overcoming her protests with the deft suggestion that she had need to be fresh in the morning.

So Adelia had obeyed, drawing a steaming tub and wallowing in unfamiliar luxury for what she knew Aunt Lettie would have considered a sinful amount of time. When at last she lay between the cool, fresh sheets, she found it impossible to relax. Her mind was full, crowded with new sensations, new images; and her body, so used to complete exhaustion before sleep, was unable to cope with the lack of physical exertion. Easing out of bed, she exchanged her nightdress for jeans and shirt and, piling her hair once more under the absurd cap, slipped noiselessly from the sleeping house.

The night was clear, cool and quiet, a vague breeze sweetening the air, only the bright, insistent call of a whippoorwill breaking the stillness. The light of the half moon guided her toward the stables as she strolled without thought of destination over the smooth new grass. The stillness, the familiar scent of animals, reminded her of home, and suddenly she felt a contentment and peace she had not even known she had lived without.

Hesitating outside the door of the large white stables, she debated whether she dare enter and spend the last of her evening with the horses. Having decided there was no harm in it, she was reaching out for the handle when an iron grip closed around her arm and whirled her around, and she was lifted off her feet for a moment like a rag doll.

"Just what do you think you're doing? And how did you get in here?"

She stared wordlessly at the owner of the harsh, angry voice, a vague shadow silhouetted in the dim moonlight, looming over her like an avenging giant.

She searched for her own voice, but the combination of shock and pain had stolen it. Her words slipped down her throat as she felt herself being dragged into the building.

"Here, let's have a look at you," the voice growled as its owner switched on the lights. He spun her around, dislodging her cap, and the glory of her hair escaped its confinement to form a fiery cascade down her back.

"What the . . . you're a girl!" He released his firm hold and Adelia stepped back and began to give him both sides of her Irish tongue.

"Sure and it's observant you are to be noticing that—" She rubbed her arm vigorously while her green eyes glared up at her astonished assailant. "And who are you to come around grabbing innocent people and crushing their bones? A great, hulking bully you are, sneaking up on a body and dragging and pulling them about! A horsewhipping is what you're deserving for scaring the life from me and nearly breaking my arm in the process—"

"You may be pint-sized, but you're packed with dynamite," the man observed, obviously amused. He wondered as he looked over her softly rounded shape how he could have mistaken her for a boy. "From your accent I could make a guess that you're little Dee, Paddy's niece."

"I'm Adelia Cunnane, but it's not your little Dee I am." She regarded him with unconcealed resentment. "And it's not me who's having the accent. It's you!"

He threw back his head and roared with laughter, increasing Adelia's fury. "Oh, I am glad to have made you so happy." Folding her arms across her chest, she tossed her head, rich dark curls swinging wildly. "And who in the world are you, I'd like to know?"

"I'm Travis," he answered, still grinning. "Travis Grant."

Chapter Two

It was Adelia's turn to gape at her companion. As the mists of fury cleared from her eyes, she saw him clearly for the first time. He was tall and powerfully built, and the sleeves of his shirt were carelessly rolled above his elbows, revealing deeply tanned, muscular arms. He had chiseled features, clear and sharp, and his eyes were so blue against the brown of his skin that they startled the casual onlooker. His hair was rich and full, thick black curls in a disarming disarray to his collar, and the mouth that continued to grin at her was well formed, showing strong white teeth.

This was the man she was to work for, this was the man she needed to impress, Adelia's brain registered numbly, and she had just raked him clean with her furious tongue. "Jakers," she whispered, shut-

ting her eyes a moment and wishing she could disappear in a puff of smoke.

"I'm sorry we met under such, uh . . ."—he hesitated, his mouth twitching again—"confusing circumstances, Adelia. Paddy's been on top of the world since he made arrangements to bring you over from Ireland."

"I didn't expect to be meeting you till tomorrow, Mr. Grant." She clung desperately to pride and kept her voice even. "Uncle Paddy said you wouldn't be back."

"I didn't expect to find a half-pint fairy invading my stables," Travis returned, grinning once again.

Adelia straightened her spine and threw him a haughty look. "I couldn't sleep, so I came for a walk. I was thinking I might look in on Majesty."

"Majesty's a very high-strung animal," Travis admonished, his gaze roaming over her from top to bottom. "You'd best keep a respectable distance."

"And how will I be doing that?" she demanded imperiously, disconcerted by his masculine appraisal. "I'm to be exercising him regularly."

"The devil you are!" His eyes rose to hers and narrowed. "If you think I'd let a slip of a thing like you on my prize colt, you've lost your senses."

"I've already been on your prize colt." Anger returned, and her head tossed with it. "I rode around your track on him in fine time."

"I don't believe it." He took a step toward her, and her head was forced to tilt still further. "Paddy wouldn't let you up on Majesty."

"I'm not in the habit of lying, Mr. Grant," Adelia

retorted with great dignity. "The boy, Tom, got a kick for his trouble, so I rode Majesty instead."

"You rode Majesty?" Travis repeated in slow, even tones.

"That I did," she agreed, then, noting the anger hardening the blue eyes, sped on. "He's a beauty, rides like the wind, but he's not bad-tempered. He wouldn't have been kicking Tom if the boy had understood him better." She was speaking rapidly, not giving Travis an opportunity to comment. "The poor thing just needed someone to talk to him, someone to show him he was loved and appreciated."

"And you can talk to horses?" Travis's lips curved on the question.

"Aye," she agreed, unaware of the mocking gleam that lit his eyes. "Anyone can if they've a mind to. I know animals, Mr. Grant. I worked with the vet back in Skibbereen, and I know a bit about healing as well. I would never do anything to bring harm to Majesty or any of your other horses. Uncle Paddy trusted me; you mustn't be angry with him."

He said nothing to this, only took his time studying her as her extraordinary eyes unknowingly employed their power. As his silence and intense regard continued, she felt a small tingle of fear, mixed with another sensation, strange and foreign, that she was unable to decipher.

"Mr. Grant," she began, swallowing pride to plead. "Please, give me a chance—a fortnight, no more." She took a deep breath and moistened her lips. "If you don't want me after that, just tell me, and I'll abide by your decision. I'll tell Uncle Paddy I'm not happy with the job, that I want to be doing something else."

"Why would you do that?" His head tilted as if to gain a new perspective.

"It's what I'd have to do," she returned with a shrug and a push at her tumbled hair. "Otherwise I'd be putting him in the middle. He's devoted to you and to this place—I know that from the letters he wrote me—but he's taken me on as his responsibility now. If I told him you had fired me, his loyalties would be torn in two. I'll not be the cause of that. Will you give me a two-week trial, Mr. Grant?" *Pride goeth before destruction,* she quoted silently, trying to remember Aunt Lettie's lectures on humility.

She stood, determined not to squirm under his silent contemplation, wishing he would not look at her as if he could read the thoughts running through her brain.

"All right, Adelia," he said at length. "You'll have your two-week trial, just between us."

A brilliant smile lit her face and she extended her hand. "Thank you, Mr. Grant. I'm grateful to you."

He accepted her hand, but his returning smile faded, a frown replacing it as he turned her palm up and examined it. Her hand was exquisitely small, fingers long and tapering, but it was rough and calloused from years of the abuse of labor. The continued contact was sending odd tingles through her body, and she looked down helplessly at the hand under his critical scrutiny.

"Is something the matter?" she asked in a voice she barely recognized.

He raised his eyes and looked into hers with an expression she could not fathom. "It's a crime for such a tiny hand to be as hard and rough as any ditchdigger's."

Unaccountably stung by his softly spoken words, she jerked her hand away, holding it behind her back. "I'm sorry they're not as soft as a lily, Mr. Grant. But it's not lady's hands I'll be needing for the job I'm doing for you. If you'll excuse me now, I'll be going in."

She moved past him quickly, and he watched her run like a rabbit across the grass and out of sight.

Birdcalls broke the night's slumber, and Adelia woke with the sun. She dressed quickly, happy with the anticipation of beginning her job, a job which was to her more of a magic wish granted than labor. She was sure she could prove herself to Travis Grant. A new home, a new life, a new beginning; she stared out at the infant sun and knew it would bring nothing but wonders.

The scent of frying bacon led Paddy to the kitchen, and he stood for a moment watching her movements while she remained unaware of his presence. She was humming an old tune he remembered from childhood, and she seemed to him the essence of shining, unspoiled youth.

"Sure and it's the most beautiful sight these old eyes have awakened to in many a year."

She turned to him, her smile dimming the sunlight

into insignificance. "Good morning to you, Uncle Paddy. It's a fine, beautiful day."

While they were eating, Adelia casually mentioned that she had met Travis Grant the previous night during her nocturnal wanderings.

"I was hoping to introduce you myself this morning." He took a bite of crisp bacon and raised his brows. "What did you think of him?"

She tactfully kept her opinion to herself and answered with a move of her shoulders. "I'm sure he's a fine, good man, Uncle Paddy, but I wasn't with him long enough to make judgments." *Big, arrogant bully,* her mind added. "But I did tell him about Tom's accident, and that I'd been taken on as an exercise boy."

"Did you, now?" A slow smile formed as he added jam to his bread. "And what did he say to that?"

"He's smart enough to trust Padrick Cunnane's opinion." Her fingers crossed under the table, and she wondered if she had earned another black mark in Aunt Lettie's often mentioned Record Book of the Angels.

A short time later, Adelia stood in front of Majesty, rubbing his muzzle and holding an intimate conversation, unaware her actions were being observed by a pair of deep blue eyes.

"Morning, Paddy. I hear you've taken on a new hand."

Paddy broke off his conversation with Hank and greeted the tall, lean man. "Good morning to you, Travis. Dee told me she met you last night."

"Did she?" His lips curved as he continued to regard woman and horse.

"Wait till you see that little lady ride," Hank put in, shaking his head. "Could have knocked me over with a feather."

Travis inclined his head. "We'll soon see." He moved to where Adelia still stood speaking softly to the large Thoroughbred. "Hello again, half-pint. Does your friend ever answer you?"

She whirled, caught off guard, and regarded his amusement with indignation. "Aye, that he does, Mr. Grant, in his own way." She brushed past him to mount, and Travis stopped her with a hand on her wrist.

"Good Lord, did I do that?" He ran a finger over the dark smudge of bruises on her arm, and Adelia followed his glance before raising her eyes to his.

"That you did."

His eyes narrowed a moment, his fingers still light on her wrist. "We'll have to be more careful with you in the future, won't we, little Dee?"

"Not the first bruising I've had, nor likely to be the last, but you'll not be having any more occasion to be grabbing at me, Mr. Grant." With this, she swung herself astride Majesty and rode him onto the track. At Paddy's signal, the pair sprinted forward and galloped around the oval in a clean, steady rhythm.

"You wouldn't have been thinking I'd lost my senses hiring my niece, now would you, lad?"

"I'll admit when she told me she'd been hired I had a moment of doubt about your sanity," Travis answered, keeping his eyes on the small woman glued to the speeding horse. "But I've always trusted your judgment, Paddy; you've never let me down."

Later that morning Adelia worked in the stables, insisting over Paddy's objections that she assist in the grooming of some of the horses. A sound behind her caused her to turn her head, and she encountered two small boys, one the mirror image of the other. She closed her eyes in mock alarm.

"Saints preserve us, sure and it's losing my mind I am! I'm seeing double."

The boys collapsed into giggles and spoke in unison. "We're twins."

"Is that the truth?" She breathed a deep sigh of relief. "Well, I'm glad to know it. I was afraid a spell had been put on me."

"You talk just like Paddy," one boy observed, eyeing her with unrestrained curiosity.

"Do I, now?" She smiled down at their identical faces. The boys were about eight, she hazarded, dark as gypsies, with snapping brown eyes. "The reason for that may be I'm his niece, Adelia Cunnane, just arrived from Ireland."

Two faces creased in two doubtful frowns. "He calls you little Dee, but you're not little, you're all grown up," one boy complained, the other nodding in agreement.

"That I am, as far as I ever will be, I'm afraid. But I was just a wee babe when I last saw Uncle Paddy, and I never did grow very tall, so I'm little Dee to him. And what might your names be?" she questioned, putting down the currycomb that she had been using.

"Mark and Mike," they announced, again in one voice.

"Don't be telling me who's who," she commanded, narrowing dark green eyes. "I'll guess; I'm mighty good at guessing." She circled them as they resumed giggling. "You'd be Mark, and you'd be Mike," she pronounced, placing a hand on each head. Two pair of eyes stared at her in amazement.

"How did you know?" Mark demanded.

"I'm Irish," she stated simply, controlling a grin. "There's many of us from Ireland who's fey."

"Fey—what's that?" Mike chimed in, eyes wide and curious.

"That means I have strange, secret powers," Adelia claimed with a dramatic sweep of her hand. The two boys looked at each other and back at Adelia, suitably impressed.

"Mark, Mike." A woman entered the stables and shook her head in despair. "I should have known the pair of you would be here."

Adelia stared at the newcomer, stunned by her beauty and elegance. She was tall and slender, clad in a simple but, to Adelia's untrained eye, overwhelmingly beautiful outfit of dark blue slacks and white silk blouse. Black, silky hair curled back from her face. Soft, rose-tinted lips and a classic straight nose led to a pair of heavily lashed deep blue eyes that Adelia identified as Travis's.

"I hope they haven't been bothering you." The woman peered down in indulgent exasperation. "They're impossible to keep track of."

"No, missus," Adelia said, wondering if there had

ever been a lovelier woman. "They're fine lads. We've just been getting acquainted."

"You must be Paddy's niece, Adelia." The generous mouth curved in a smile.

"Aye, missus." Adelia managed a smile of her own and wondered what it would be like to be as graceful as a willow limb.

"I'm Trish Collins, Travis's sister." She extended her hand, and Adelia gaped at it in horror. After Travis's words of the previous night she was self-conscious about the state of her hands, and her mind began to work swiftly.

How could she put her hard, rough hand into such a lovely soft one! Yet there was no way out without being pointedly rude, so, wiping her palm on her jeans, she joined it with the one Trish offered. The other woman had noted Adelia's hesitation and concluded the reason for it when their hands met, but she made no comment.

At that moment, Travis entered the building, along with Paddy and a small, spare man Adelia did not recognize.

"Paddy!" The twins launched themselves at the stocky figure.

"Well, if it isn't Tweedledee and Tweedledum. And what mischief have you been up to this fine day?"

"We came to meet Dee," Mark announced. "She guessed which one of us was which."

"She's fey," Mike added soberly.

Paddy nodded, equally grave, his eyes twinkling as they met Adelia's over the two small heads. "Aye, that's a fact. There's been many a Cunnane who's had the sight."

"Adelia Cunnane"—Travis made introductions, a light smile playing over his mouth—"Dr. Robert Loman, our vet."

"Pleased to meet you, Doctor," Adelia greeted him, strategically keeping her hands behind her back.

"Rob's come to look over Solomy," Paddy explained. "She'll be foaling soon."

The pixie face lit with pleasure, and, looking down at her, Travis raised his brows. "Would you like to see her, Adelia?"

"Very much." She beamed him a smile, previous animosity forgotten.

"She's foaling quite late," Travis commented as the group walked down the long length of stalls. "A Thoroughbred's official birthday is January the first, and normally we breed with that in mind. We just acquired Solomy six months ago, and of course she was already in foal. She's from a good line, and the stud she was bred to is by the same sire as Majesty."

"Then you must have big hopes for the foal," Adelia returned, thinking of Majesty's style and speed.

"I think," he said with a smile, "you could safely say we had hopes for this foal." Placing a hand on her shoulder, he turned her toward an enclosure. "Adelia," Travis said with amused formality, "meet Solomy."

She sighed with delight at the animal, a dark, gleaming bay mare with a mane of flowing black silk.

Running her hand down the stark flash of white on the forehead, she looked into dark, intelligent eyes.

"You're a fine, beautiful lady." The caressing of the smooth hide was met with a whinny of approval.

"I suppose you'd like a closer look," Travis observed, opening the stall door and gesturing for her to enter.

She preceded him and the vet into the stall, carrying on a low conversation with Solomy as she explored the swollen belly, probing with gentle, capable fingers. After a few moments she stopped and turned concerned eyes to Travis's laughing ones.

"The foal's turned wrong."

The blue eyes lost their laughter and studied her intently.

"Quite right, Miss Cunnane," Robert Loman agreed with a professional nod. "A quick diagnosis." Entering the stall, he too ran hands over the mare's belly. "We're hoping the foal will turn before she's full term."

"But you're not thinking it's likely; her time's almost here."

"No, we're not." He turned back to her, faintly surprised and greatly curious as to her knowledge. "We have to deal with the possibility of a breech. Have you had any training?"

"More doing than training." She shrugged, uncomfortable at having the attention focused on her. "I worked with a vet back in Ireland. I've done some birthings and some stitching and splinting."

She stepped out of the stall to stand beside Paddy, watching as the vet proceeded with his work.

Paddy's arm slipped around her shoulders, and she rested her head against him.

"I hate to think what a hard time she'll be having. We had a mare that carried breech once, and I had to turn the babe." She sighed with the memory. "I can still see her poor, trusting eyes on me. How I hated to hurt her."

"You turned a foal by yourself?" Travis demanded, drawing her attention from the past. "That's a difficult enough job for a full-grown man, let alone a little thing like you."

She bristled, bringing herself up to the full of her meager height. "It may be that I'm small, Mr. Grant, but I'm strong enough to do what needs to be done." She glared up at him, her pride under attack, and stuck out her chin. "I'll tell you this: for all our difference in size I can work the day through with you!"

Stifling a snort of laughter, Paddy focused on a spot on the ceiling as Travis regarded her indignation with cool, steady eyes. After a moment, she turned and began to walk toward the front of the building.

"Did you really see a horse being born, Dee?" The twins tagged after her full of excitement.

"Many a time, and cows and pigs and the like." She took a small hand in each of hers and continued over the concrete floor. "There was a time I birthed twin lambs, and that was the prettiest sight . . ."

Travis continued to stare after her as her voice trailed off in the distance.

The next few days passed easily for Adelia as she became accustomed to a new life and new surroundings. On the occasions she spoke to Travis, she continually struggled to hold back the tongue he seemed to have a habit of provoking. He stirred strange feelings in her, feelings she could neither comprehend nor prevent, and her defense against them took shape in a quick retort and flashing eyes. Though she gave herself nightly lectures on the evils of temper, when confronted with him during the daylight hours her vow of restraint slipped through her fingers.

She found herself watching him once as he strode toward the stables, his blue denim work shirt straining over broad shoulders as he moved over the grass. He seemed to eat up the ground with a careless vitality. There was a strange pull at her heart, and she sighed, then bit her lip in annoyance. It was only that he was such a fine, strongly built man, she told herself, lean and powerful. She dismounted from the Thoroughbred she had been exercising and rubbed his neck vigorously. She had always admired strength and power, the same way she admired this strong, well-proportioned animal. Everyone she had met held Travis Grant in great respect and admiration. When he gave an order, it was carried out without question. Only Paddy, it seemed, had the right to advise or question.

But she was Adelia Cunnane, she reminded herself, and no man would get the better of her. She would not play peasant to his squire and pull her forelock when he passed by. She did her job, and did it well. He would have no cause to complain in that field. But she would speak her piece if she'd a mind to, and the devil take him if he didn't like it!

Late each afternoon, Adelia visited Solomy. She was sure the mare would deliver any day, and, knowing the birth would be a difficult one, she spent her visits comforting the mare and gaining her confidence.

"Soon you'll be having a fine, strong son or daughter," Adelia told her as she closed the stall door after her visit. "I'd like to take you and the babe and bundle you off with me. What do you think himself would do about that?"

"He might be tempted to have you hanged for horse thieving."

She spun around, her eyes encountering Travis's powerful form resting idly against the next stall. "It's a bad habit you have of sneaking up and scaring a body to death," she snapped at him, assuming that the uneven beat of her heart was the result of surprise.

"I do happen to own this place, Adelia," he returned in low, calm tones that only increased her agitation.

"That's a fact I'm not likely to forget. There's no need to remind me." She tilted her chin in defiance of him and the continuing flutter of her stomach, knowing she should guard her words, and knowing the power to do so was beyond her. "I give you your day's work, but maybe you think I'm forgetting my place. Should I be bobbing a curtsy, Mr. Grant?"

"You impudent little wench," Travis muttered, straightening from his relaxed position. "I'm getting a bit weary of being stabbed by that sharp tongue of yours."

"Well, it's sorry I am about that. The best advice I can give is that you not be conversing with me."

"That's the best idea you've had." He grabbed her around the waist, lifting her a foot off the ground as their eyes warred with each other. "I've been wanting to do this since the first time you slashed at me with your sharp Irish tongue."

He crushed her mouth with his, cutting off a heated retort. Too surprised by his action to resist immediately, Adelia began to experience unfamiliar and disturbing sensations, a heat and weakness that she might feel on a day spent working in the field. His hands were like steel around her small waist, holding her body suspended in the air while his lips assaulted hers, entering her mouth with his tongue in a kiss that was both devastating and totally foreign to any she had ever known.

Pressed hard against him, lips joined, she felt his warmth, his essence, seeping into her, demanding and receiving her merging. She could feel the authority in the arms that held her, taste the knowledge on the lips that claimed hers, and body and mind surrendered to both. Unable to combat the turbulence of the unexplored, she felt it whirl her like a cyclone, spinning her toward the sun until the heat threatened to become fire.

And as each of her senses were assaulted and conquered, he continued to explore her mouth, feasting on it as a man who knew a woman's flavor. He took, and she knew nothing of the richness of the banquet she gave him, warm and ripe and fresh.

After a lifetime, he released her, dropping her back to the ground as she stared at him mutely, eyes huge with confusion.

"Well, half-pint, this is the first time I've seen you at a loss for words." He mocked her openly, the lips that had just conquered hers lifted in a smug, satisfied smile.

His taunt broke the strange hold over her mind and tongue, and her eyes lit with molten green fire. "You son of the devil," she began in a rich explosion, and what followed was a raging stream of Irish curses and dire predictions delivered in so strong an accent that it was nearly impossible to comprehend the words.

When her imagination had at last run dry, and she could only stand staring at him breathlessly, he threw back his head and laughed until she thought he would burst.

"Oh, Dee, you're a fabulous sight when you're breathing fire!" He took no trouble to hide his amusement, an infuriating grin glued to his face. "The madder you get, the thicker the brogue. I'm going to have to provoke you more often."

"I'm giving you warning," she returned in an ominous voice, which only widened the grin. "If you ever molest me again, it's more than my tongue you'll be feeling."

Lifting her head, she strode out of the stables, clutching the last threads of her dignity around her.

She said nothing to Paddy about her scene with Travis, and instead banged around the kitchen as she prepared dinner, muttering incoherent sentences about great arrogant beasts and strong-arm bullies. Her fury with Travis was intermingled with fury with herself. The fact that his touch had brought both excitement and unexplained pleasure angered her further, and she berated herself for the uncontrollable attraction she felt for him.

Chapter Three

By the next day, Adelia's anger had faded. She was not given to prolonged periods of ill humor; rather, she exploded like a burst of flame, simmered, then slowly cooled down. There remained, however, a disturbing new awareness, an awareness both of herself and the unfamiliar longings of womanhood, and of the frustrating, attractive man who had released them.

She managed to avoid any face-to-face contact with Travis during the morning, going about her duties in the normal fashion while she kept a cautious eye alert for his approach. Duties complete, she strolled back for her daily visit with Solomy. Instead of leaning over the low barrier to greet her, as was Solomy's habit, Adelia found her lying on her side in the hay, breathing heavily.

"By all the saints and apostles!" Rushing inside,

she knelt beside the raggedly breathing mare. "Your time's come, darlin'," she crooned, running her hands over the large mounded belly. "Just rest easy now. I'll be back." Springing up, she sped from the stables.

She spotted Tom in the far paddock and, cupping her hands, shouted. "Solomy's time's here. Get Travis—call the vet. Be quick!" Without waiting for an answer, she ran back inside to comfort the laboring horse.

She was murmuring and stroking the sweating hide when Travis and Paddy joined her. Soft words and gentle hands had calmed the mare, whose deep brown eyes were riveted on Adelia's dark green ones.

Travis knelt beside her, his hand joining hers on the gleaming skin, and though Adelia spoke to him, her eyes never left the mare's.

"The foal's still the wrong way; it must be turned, and quickly. Where's Dr. Loman?"

"He's had an emergency—can't be here for half an hour." His voice was clipped, his own attention on Solomy.

She turned her head and captured his gaze. "Mr. Grant, I'm telling you she doesn't have that long. The foal has to be turned now, or we'll lose them both. I can do it; I've done it before. It's God's truth, Mr. Grant, she hasn't much time."

They stared at each other for a long moment, Adelia's eyes wide and pleading, his narrowed and intense. Solomy let out an agonizing whinny as a new contraction began.

"There, my love." Adelia switched her attention back to the mare, murmuring words of comfort.

"All right," Travis agreed, a long breath escaping through his teeth. "But I'll turn it. Paddy, call in some of the men to hold her down."

"No!" Adelia's protest caused the mare to start, and she spoke quietly again, using hands and voice to soothe. "You'll not bring a bunch of bruisers in here forcing her down and frightening her." Again she raised her eyes to Travis's and spoke with calm assurance. "She'll hold for me; I know how."

"Travis," Paddy intervened as he started to speak. "Dee knows what she's about." Nodding, Travis moved off to scrub his hands and arms.

"Have a care," she warned as he prepared to begin. "The babe's hooves will be sharp, and the womb can close on your hand quickly." Taking a deep breath, she lay her cheek against the mare's, hands circling the damp flesh in a steady rhythm as she began to croon in quiet Gaelic.

The mare shivered as Travis entered her, but remained still listening to Adelia's comforting voice.

The air seemed to grow closer, heavy with Solomy's breathing and the mystical beauty of the ancient tongue Adelia murmured. It brought a heavy warmth to the spring afternoon, isolating them from all but the struggle for life.

"I've got him," Travis announced, sweat running unheeded down his face. His breath came quickly, and he muttered a steady stream of soft curses, but Adelia heard nothing, giving herself over to the mare. "It's done." He rested back on his heels, turning his attention to the woman at his side. She gave no sign to him, only continued her slow, rhythmic crooning, hands gently caressing, face buried in the mare's neck.

"Here it comes," Paddy cried, and she turned her head to watch the miracle of birth. When the foal finally emerged into the world, both woman and horse sighed and shuddered.

"It's a fine, strong son you have, Solomy. Ah, sure, and there's no more beautiful sight in the world than an innocent new life!"

She turned her glowing face to Travis and gave him a smile that rivaled the sun. Their eyes met, and the look deepened until it seemed to Adelia that time had stopped. She felt herself being drawn into fathoms of dark blue, unable to breathe or speak, as if some invisible shield had descended, insulating them from all but each other.

Can love come in an instant? her numbed brain demanded. Or has it been there forever? The answer was forestalled as Robert Loman arrived, shattering the magic that had held her suspended.

She stood up quickly as the vet began to question Travis on the colt's delivery. A wave of giddiness washed over her as she rose, and she sank her teeth into her lower lip to combat the weakness. Keeping the mare calm had been an enormous strain, almost as if she had experienced each pang of labor, and the unexpected rush of emotion when Travis had held her eyes had left her drained and dizzy.

"What is it, Dee?" Paddy's voice was full of concern as he took her arm.

"Nothing." She placed her palm to her spinning head. "Just a bit of a headache."

"Take her home," Travis commanded, regarding her closely. Her eyes were bright and enormous against her pallor, and she appeared suddenly small and helpless. Rising, he moved toward her, and she stepped back, terrified he would touch her.

"There's no need." She kept her voice calm and even. "I'll just go up and have a wash. I'm fine, Uncle Paddy." She smiled into his frowning face, avoiding Travis's at all costs. "Don't you worry." Stepping from the stall, she moved quickly from the building, filling her lungs with fresh, clean air.

That evening found Adelia quiet and pensive. She was unused to confusion and uncertainty, characteristically knowing what needed to be done and doing it. Her life had always been basic, the fundamental existence of meeting demands as they came. There had been no room for indecision or clouded reasoning in a world that was essentially black or white.

She lingered in the kitchen after dinner, reasoning with herself with firm common sense. The foaling had been difficult, the strain emptying her body of its strength, and the sight of the new colt had fogged her brain. These were the reasons she had reacted so strongly to Travis. She could hardly be in love with him; she barely knew him, and what she did know was not altogether to her taste. He was too big, too strong, too self-confident, and too arrogant. He reminded her of a feudal lord, and Adelia was too Irish to have any liking for landed gentry.

However, after her work was done and self-analysis complete, she remained oddly weary and disturbed. Sitting down on the floor at Paddy's feet, she laid her head in his lap with a deep sigh.

"Little Dee," he murmured, stroking the thick auburn curls. "You're working too hard."

"What nonsense," she disagreed, snuggling deeper into the still newness of comfort. "I haven't worked a full day since I arrived. The day would not nearly be over yet if I was back on the farm."

"Was it hard for you, lass?" he asked, thinking she might now be ready to talk of it.

Again Adelia sighed, moving her shoulders restlessly. "I wouldn't say hard, Uncle Paddy, but everything changed after Mother and Da died."

"Poor little Dee, such a wee thing to be losing so much."

"I thought my world had ended when they died," she whispered, hardly aware she was speaking aloud. "I'm thinking I died myself for a time, so angry and frightened I was, then numb, feeling nothing. But I began remembering how they were together. No two people could have loved each other more. Such a fine, full loving they had, even a child could see it."

So engrossed were the man and woman in the words being spoken that neither heard the sound of feet climbing the stairs. Travis halted in his action of knocking, dropping his hand as he watched the poignant picture, and Adelia's words drifted through the screen.

"The only thing I could give them was the farm, and it was all I had left of them. Poor Aunt Lettie, she worked so hard, and I was a constant cross for her to bear." She laughed as memory flickered through her mind. "She never could understand why I had to ride so fast. 'Sure and it's your neck you'll be breaking,' she used to call after me, shaking her fist. 'Who'll be helping with the plowing if you bash in your head on the road?' Then when I'd have one of my rages and go off shouting and cursing— and it's often, I'm afraid I did just that—she'd cross herself and start praying for my doomed soul.

"Jakers, but we worked." With a long breath she shut her eyes. "But it was too much for one woman and a half-grown girl, and not enough money to hire help, and none to be made without it. Do you know how it is, Uncle Paddy, when you see the thing you need, but the closer you get the further away it is? Always moving away from you, always just out of your reach. Sometimes, when I look back, I can't tell one day from the rest. Then Aunt Lettie had that stroke, and how she hated to be lying there helpless day after day."

"Why did you never let me know how things were?" Paddy questioned, looking down at her dark head. "I could have helped you—sent you money, or come back myself."

She raised her head and smiled at him. "Aye, that's just what you would have done, and to what good? Throwing your money away, taking yourself from the life you'd chosen . . . I'd not have had that for a minute, and neither would Aunt Lettie, or Mother and Da. The farm's gone, just as they are, and so is Ireland. Now I have you, I'm not needing another thing."

Looking into his eyes, seeing the concern and regret written there, she wished suddenly she had kept her own counsel. "How is it, Padrick Cunnane, that a fine, handsome man like yourself never took a wife?" Her grin turned impish, and devils danced in her eyes. "There must have been dozens of ladies willing. Have you never found a woman to love?"

He touched her cheek, giving her a wistful smile. "Aye, lass, that I did, but she chose your father."

Deep green eyes filled with surprise that melted into sympathy. "Oh, Uncle Paddy!" She flung her arms around him, and Travis turned from the door and walked silently down the stairs.

The next morning the air seemed to sigh with spring, whispering promises of flowers and cool, leafy trees. To Adelia it brought memories of other springs. Spring was the time the earth asked to be replenished and grew pregnant with new life. Her world had always revolved around the earth, its gifts and hardships, its demands and promises.

From the balcony of Paddy's house she surveyed the land that was Travis's. It seemed to stretch on and on with the easy, gentle roll of a calm sea. Green and brown waves were dotted, not with boats, but with finely sculptured Thoroughbreds. It ran through her mind that she had no conception of what lay over the last hill. This land was still a stranger. From the moment of her arrival in America she had seen little else but what belonged to Travis Grant.

Over the pure, sweet air floated an occasional whinny or the quick call of a bird. But for this, there was silence. There was no strident call of rooster announcing the new day, no fields turned up waiting to receive seed, no weeds demanding uprooting. All at once homesickness washed over her so intensely that she could only shut her eyes and weather the storm.

So much is gone, she thought, and her hands hugged her elbows as if in comfort. I'll never be able to go back, never see the farm again. Sighing, she opened her eyes and tried to shake off the melancholy. There's nothing to be done about it; the bridges are burned. This is home now, and if it's not really mine, it's the closest I'll come.

"Where are you, lass?"

Adelia started slightly as Paddy's arm slipped around her; then she sighed again and rested against his shoulder. "Back on the farm, I suppose. Thinking about spring planting."

"It's a day for it, isn't it? The air's cool, and the sun's warm." He gave her shoulder a small squeeze, then clucked his tongue as if in regret. "I've got to go into town today. It's a pity."

"A pity?"

"I was hoping to get some seeds in around the walkway. Thought I might make a flower bed in front of the house too." He shook his head and sighed. "Just don't know when I'll find the time."

"Oh, I'll do it, Uncle Paddy. I've plenty of time." Drawing away, she looked at him with such innocent acceptance of his trumped-up excuse that he nearly broke into a grin.

"Little Dee, I couldn't ask you to do all that on your day off." He creased his face into doubtful lines and patted her cheek. "No, it's too much. I'll get to it as soon as I find a bit of time."

"Uncle Paddy, don't be silly. I'd love to do it." Her smile was blooming again, chasing the clouds from her eyes. "Just show me what you want done."

"Well . . ." He permitted her to argue a few more minutes before allowing himself to be persuaded.

Armed with a myriad of seed packs and a small spade, Adelia stood on the patch of lawn surrounding Paddy's house and mentally mapped out her landscaping. Petunias along the walk, asters and marigolds against the house, impatiens for the border. And sweet peas, she thought with a smile, for the trellis she had asked Paddy to buy. In the fall, she decided, I'll plant bulbs, as many as the ground will hold. Daffodils and tulips. Satisfied with her planning, she began to turn the earth.

The sun grew warmer, and her sleeves were soon pushed past her elbows. In the distance she could hear the sounds of men and horses going through their daily routine: a shout, laughter, the thud of hooves on dirt. But soon, lost in her planting, she drifted apart. Softly, she began to sing a song remembered from childhood, the words soothing and familiar. The scent of fresh earth eased the ache with which she had awakened.

A shadow fell across her. Twisting her head, she dropped the spade nervously as Travis looked down at her.

"I've made you stop. I'm sorry."

He seemed impossibly tall as he stood over her. She craned her neck and squinted against the sun. It glowed in an aura around his head, and for one fanciful moment she thought he looked like a knight on his way to vanquish dragons.

"No, you just startled me." Picking up the spade, Adelia told herself she was a fool and began to work again.

"I didn't mean the planting." He crouched down beside her, his shoulder brushing hers. "I mean the song. It sounded very old and very sad."

"Aye, it's both." She inched away, carefully patting soil over seeds. "A lot of Gaelic songs are old and sad."

Folding his legs under him, he sat easily on the grass and watched her. "What's it about?"

"Oh, love, of course. The saddest songs are always about love." She lifted her head to smile at him. His face was close, his mouth a breath away. The spade hung suspended in her hand as she only stared, wondering what she would do if the whisper of space was gone and his mouth found hers.

"Is love always sad, Adelia?" His voice was as soft as the breeze that danced around them.

"I don't know. I . . ." She felt the weakness growing stronger and tore her eyes from his. "We were talking about songs."

"So we were," Travis murmured, then brushed back the hair that curtained her face. She swallowed and began digging with renewed interest. "I never thanked you properly for your help yesterday with Solomy."

"Oh, well . . ." Moving her shoulders, she kept her eyes on the ground. "I didn't do that much. I'm just glad Solomy and the foal are well. Do you like flowers, Mr. Grant?" she asked, needing to change the subject.

"Yes, I like flowers. What are you planting?" His voice was casual as he lifted a package of seeds.

"All different kinds," she told him, this time able to raise her head and smile. "They'll be a lovely sight by summer. Your soil's rich, Mr. Grant; it wants to give." She squeezed a handful of earth, then held it out in her palm.

"You'd know more about that than I." Taking her fingertips, he studied the soil in her hand. "You're the farmer."

"I was," she amended and tried to free her hand.

"I'm afraid I don't know much about planting—vegetables or flowers." He ignored her attempts to pull her fingers away and brought his eyes to hers. "I suppose it's a gift."

"It just takes time and effort, like anything else. Here." Concluding that if she gave him something to do her hand would be released, she held out some seeds. "Just drop a few in and cover them up. Don't crowd them," she instructed as he obeyed. "They want room to spread. Now you cover them up and let nature take over." Smiling, she absently brushed a hand across her cheek. "No matter what you do, nature has the last word in any case. A farmer knows that here the same way a farmer knows that in Ireland."

"So, now that I've put them in," he concluded with a grin, "I just sit back and watch them grow."

"Well," she said, tilting her head and giving him a sober stare, "there might be a thing or two more, like watering or weeding. These seeds will take quick, and the flowers will pop up before you know it. I'm putting in sweet peas there." She pointed across the lawn, forgetting that she still held the soil in her other hand. "When the breeze comes up at night, the scent will drift through the windows. There's something special about sweet peas. They start off so small, but they'll just keep climbing as long as there's something to hold on to. There should be a rose-bush," she murmured almost to herself. "When the scents mingle together, it's like nothing else on earth. Red roses, just starting to open up."

"Are you homesick, Dee?" The question was low and gentle, but her head whipped back around in surprise.

"I . . ." Shrugging, she bent her face to her work again, uncomfortable that he had read her emotions so clearly.

"It's quite natural." He lifted her chin with his hand until their eyes met again. "It's not easy to leave behind everything you've ever known."

"No." Moving her shoulders again, she turned away and began to spread marigold seeds. "But I made the choice, and it truly was what I wanted. It's what I want," she amended with more firmness. "I can't say I've been unhappy a moment since I got off the plane. I can't go back, and I don't really know if I'd want to if I could. I've a new life now." Tossing back her hair, she smiled at him. "I like it here. The people, the work, the horses, the land." Her hand made a wide, encompassing gesture. "You've a beautiful home, Mr. Grant; anyone could be happy here."

He brushed a trace of dirt from her cheek and

returned her smile. "I'm glad you think so, but it's your home too."

"You're a generous man, Mr. Grant." She kept her gaze level with his, but her smile was suddenly sad and sweet. "There's not many who'd say that and mean it, and I'm grateful to you. But for better or worse, the farm was mine." Sighing, she traced a finger through the soil. "It was mine. . . ."

Late the next morning when Adelia turned one of the Thoroughbreds she had been exercising over to a groom, Trish Collins approached her with a friendly smile. "Hello, Adelia. How are you settling in?"

"Fine, missus, and good morning to you." She regarded Trish's dark beauty with fresh admiration. "And where are the lads this morning?"

"In school, but they'll be here tomorrow. They're half crazy to get a look at the new foal."

"A beautiful sight he is."

"Yes, I've just had a peek at him. Travis told me how marvelous you were with the mare."

Her mouth dropped open a moment, surprised and inordinately pleased that Travis should have praised her. "I was glad to help, missus. Solomy did all the work."

"Call me Trish," she requested with a shake of her head. "Missus makes me feel old and crotchety."

"Oh, no, missus, you're not old at all," she blurted out, horrified.

"I wouldn't like to think so. Travis and I won't be thirty-one until October." Trish laughed at the stricken face.

"So you're twins as well," Adelia concluded,

feeling more at ease. "I suppose that's why I saw your brother's eyes the first time I met you."

"Yes, we do bear a strong resemblance to each other, which is why I constantly tell him how handsome he is." She smiled at Adelia's light, musical laugh. "Am I holding you up? Are you busy?"

"No, missus." At the raised brow, she amended, "No, Trish. I was about to take my break and fix a cup of tea. Would you like one?"

"Yes, thank you, I would."

They paused at the top of the stairs to the garage house as Adelia bent to pick up a long, narrow white box. "Now what might this be?"

"Flowers would be my guess," Trish concluded, indicating the printed name of a local florist.

"What would they be doing here?" She frowned down at the box as they stepped inside. "Someone must have left them at the wrong house."

"You might open them and find out," Trish suggested, amused by the frown of concentration. "As your name's on the box, they just might be for you."

Auburn curls danced as she shook her head and chuckled. "Now who'd be sending me flowers?" Setting the box on a table, she opened the lid and gave a small cry of pleasure. "Oh, just look! Have you ever seen such a sight?" The box was filled with long-stemmed roses, deep blood red, their half-closed petals soft as velvet to her hesitant fingers. Lifting one out, she held it under her nose. "Ah," she breathed and passed the bloom to Trish. "Straight from heaven." Then, shrugging, she re-

turned to practical matters. "Who could they be
for?"

"There should be a card."

Locating the small white note, Adelia read it
silently, and her green eyes widened as she read the
words a second time. She brought her gaze from the
slip of paper to meet an openly curious regard.
"They're for me." Her voice mirrored disbelief as
she handed Trish the card. "Your brother sent them
to thank me for helping with Solomy."

"'Dee, to thank you for your help with the new
foal. Travis,'" Trish read aloud, and added under
her breath, "You certainly wax poetic on occasion,
brother."

"In my whole life," Adelia murmured, touching a
silky petal, "no one has ever given me flowers."

Trish looked over quickly, observing the shimmering eyes and the stunned pleasure passing over
Adelia's features. Pushing tears back, Adelia spoke
on a sigh. "This was a lovely thing for your brother
to do. I had a rosebush at home—red roses they
were too. My mother planted it." She smiled, feeling
incredibly happy. "It makes them that much more
special."

Later, they walked back to the stables. As they
drew near, Travis and Paddy emerged from the
building, and the Irishman greeted them both with a
beaming smile.

"Travis, we've died and gone to heaven. Sure and
it's two angels coming to greet us."

"Uncle Paddy." Adelia tweaked his cheek. "Living in America hasn't lessened your gift for blar-

ney." Looking up at the man who towered above the rest of them, she treated him to the pure, honest smile of a child. "I want to thank you for the flowers, Mr. Grant. They're lovely."

"I'm glad you liked them," he answered, enjoying the smile. "It was little enough after what you did."

"Here's something more for you, Dee." Paddy reached into his pocket and withdrew a piece of paper. "Your first week's wages."

"Oh," Adelia said with a grin. "It's the first time I've been paid in money for doing anything." She frowned at the check, confused, and Travis's brows rose in amusement at her expression.

"Is something wrong with it, Adelia?"

"Yes . . . no . . . I . . ." she stumbled and brought her eyes to Paddy.

"You're wondering what it is in pounds," he concluded, grinning merrily.

"I don't think I figured it right," she answered, embarrassed under Travis's gaze.

Chuckling, he did some mental arithmetic and told her. Confusion changed to astonishment and something close to terror.

"What would I be doing with that kind of money?"

"First time anyone around here complained about being overpaid," Travis commented and received a baleful glance.

"Here." Adelia turned her attention back to her uncle and held the check out to him. "You take it."

"Now, why would I be doing that, Dee? It's your money; you earned it."

"But I've never had so much money at one time in my whole life." She sent him a pleading look. "What will I do with it?"

"Go out and buy some of those female trappings and folderol," he suggested vaguely, waving his hand, then pushing the check back at her. "Treat yourself to something. The good Lord knows it's about time."

"But, Uncle Paddy—"

"Why don't you buy yourself a dress, Dee?" Travis inserted with a grin. "I'm curious to see if you've got legs under those jeans."

Adelia's head snapped up, and she eyed Travis with a dangerous gleam. "Aye, I've legs, Mr. Grant, and I've been told a time or two it's not a trial to look at them. But you'll not have to be worrying yourself; it's not dresses I need to tend your horses."

His grin only widened as he gave a negligent shrug. "It doesn't matter to me if you want to be taken for a boy."

Her wrath increased as he had meant it to, and her eyes fired sharp green daggers. "There's only one who ever made that mistake, he being an ill-mannered, bad-tempered brute of a man without a brain working in his empty head."

"Shopping's a marvelous idea," Trish broke in, deciding it was time to play peacemaker. "As a matter of fact, Travis"—she smiled and fluttered her lashes—"Dee's taking the rest of the day off so we can do just that."

"Oh, really?" he returned dryly, folding his arms across his chest.

"Yes, *really*. Come on, Dee."

"But I haven't finished. . . ."

Trish linked her arm through the still protesting Adelia's and propelled her to a late-model compact. Before she had time to think things through, Adelia had an account at a local bank, a checkbook, and more cash than her apprehensive brain could comprehend.

"Now"—Trish backed the compact from its parking space—"we're going shopping."

"But what will I buy?" She stared at Trish's clear profile in complete consternation.

Stopping at a red light, Trish turned to her anxious face. "When's the last time you bought something for yourself for the fun of it? Have you ever bought something because you wanted it instead of just needing it?" The light changed, and as she joined the flow of traffic she sighed at Adelia's blank expression. "Don't misunderstand. I'm not saying people should just throw their money away, but it's high time you did something for yourself." Glancing at Adelia's furrowed brow, she smiled and shook her head. "You can afford to slow down, Dee, take a day off, buy something foolish, stretch your wings, take a breath." She grinned as Adelia merely stared at her. "The sky will not fall if Adelia Cunnane takes time off to have some fun."

No one was more surprised than Adelia when, in fact, she did have fun. The large mall fascinated her with its various small specialty shops and large department stores. There were more clothes than she had ever seen, in colors and soft materials that had her staring and touching in frank admiration. While Adelia gazed around her, Trish examined garments critically, going from rack to rack, dismissing dozens of dresses, skirts, and blouses, occasionally removing an item and hanging it over her arm. Finding herself in a changing room, Adelia could only stare at the garments Trish had placed on a hook. Then, taking a deep breath, she stripped off her shirt and jeans and slipped on a soft jersey dress in muted shades of green.

The silky material felt strange and wonderful to her skin, clinging to gentle curves and falling gracefully below her knees. She gaped at the stranger in the mirror, her hand seeking the cross at her throat to assure herself that she was still the same person.

"Dee," Trish called from outside the curtain, "have you got one on yet?"

"Aye," she answered slowly, and Trish pulled the curtain aside, smiling in triumph at the reflection in the full-length mirror.

"I knew that dress was you the minute I saw it."

"It doesn't feel like me," Adelia mumbled, then turned to face Trish directly. "It's beautiful, but what would I do with so grand a dress? I exercise horses. I work in a stable—"

"Dee," Trish interrupted firmly. "Whatever your occupation, you're still a human being; you're still a woman, an exceptionally beautiful woman." Adelia's eyes widened, and her mouth opened to protest, but before the words could be uttered Trish took her by the shoulders and turned her to face her reflection. "Look at yourself, really look," she ordered in no-nonsense terms, then shifted to gentler tones. "There'll be times when you'll want only to be a woman; this dress is for those times. Now," she said with practical authority as she released her, "try something else on."

For the rest of the afternoon Adelia allowed Trish to take command. For the first time in more than a decade, she permitted someone else to make all the decisions, and somehow she found she was having fun. They halted in front of a cosmetics counter, and Trish began spraying scents until Adelia grumbled in protest.

"This." Trish selected one of the bottles she had sampled. "Light and delicate, with just a touch of spirit." Paying for the cologne, she handed the package to Adelia. "A present."

"Oh, but I can't!"

"Yes, you can. Friends get pleasure from giving presents. Now, that marvelous skin of yours doesn't need any help, but I think we'll accent your eyes— and some lipstick, nothing too dramatic." She stopped and laughed. "I'm bullying you, aren't I?"

"Aye," Adelia agreed, feeling caught up in a genial whirlwind and finding she liked it.

"Well, you needed it," Trish said firmly. "Is there anything else you want?"

She hesitated, then blurted out quickly. "Something for my hands. Your brother said I've hands like a ditchdigger's."

"That man!" she exclaimed in disgust. "He's the epitome of tact and diplomacy."

"Trish, hello!"

Adelia turned to see a flash of amazing silver-blond hair before Trish was enveloped in an exuberant embrace. Adelia's first startled impression was of lavish curls and musky scent.

"I'm so glad to see you, darling." A high, bubbly voice drifted with the scent. "It's been weeks."

"Hello, Laura." With an affectionate smile, Trish disentangled herself. "It's good to see you too. Laura Bowers—Adelia Cunnane."

"How do you do, Mistress Bowers." The greeting was returned with a flash of beautiful white teeth before Laura's attention returned to Trish.

"Darling, how is that fabulous brother of yours?"

"Fabulous," Trish returned, giving Adelia a quick grin of mischief.

"Don't tell me he's not pining after Margot?" Laura sighed and gave a flutter of extensive lashes. "I was so hoping to offer him my comfort. Not even a tear or two to be dried?"

"He seems to be bearing up under the strain," Trish returned. Hearing the unexpected sarcasm, Adelia glanced at her in surprise.

"Oh, well, if he doesn't need comfort," Laura continued, obviously not affected by Trish's tone, "he's still at loose ends, so to speak. If dear Margot overplayed her hand by whisking off to Europe, I for one am not above volunteering to fill the gap. Heard from her lately?"

"Not a peep."

"Well, then, I'll take it that no news is good news." She gave Trish a wink and tossed her brilliant curls. "Such a gorgeous man. Do you know Travis, Adelaide?"

"Adelia," Trish corrected before Adelia could do so herself. "Yes, Dee knows Travis very well."

"Charming man," Laura bubbled. "Now that Margot's out of the picture, at least temporarily, I'll just have to give him a ring. Do tell him I'll call, won't you?" With another flurry of curls, she pecked both of Trish's cheeks. "I hate to, darling, but I simply must run. Don't forget to give Travis my very best. So nice to have met you, Amanda."

Adelia opened her mouth, then closed it again as Laura scurried off in a wave of musk.

"Sorry, Amanda." Trish grinned and patted Adelia's cheek. "Laura's really very sweet and basically kind, but she's a bit short of brains."

"She has such beautiful hair." Tearing her gaze from Laura's retreating coiffure, Adelia turned back to Trish. "I've never seen hair that color before. She must be very proud of it."

Trish laughed until she was forced to wipe away tears as Adelia looked on in puzzlement. "Oh, Dee, I adore you! Come on, we'll get that hand cream; then I'll buy you a cup of tea."

Waiting patiently while her mentor weighed the pros and cons of various lotions, Adelia reflected on Laura Bowers's conversation. *Margot,* she repeated, nibbling absently on her bottom lip. Who is this Margot, and what is she to Travis? For a moment she struggled with the urge to ask Trish outright, then, remembering her manners, she kept silent. *Perhaps he's in love with her.* This thought brought such a sharp, unexpected pain that she nearly gasped aloud. *But he's not,* a part of her insisted. If Travis Grant were ever to love a woman he would never let her go. He would go to the ends of the earth to bring her back. Unless, of course, *he had been rejected.* His pride would never allow him to pursue a woman who had refused him. But who would ever refuse such a man? *It's not my concern,* she told herself fiercely, forcing herself to concentrate on Trish's detailed description of various hand lotions.

At last Trish was satisfied. Adelia was suitably outfitted and had all the cosmetics that Trish thought were necessary. Laden with parcels, the two women headed back to the car. For once, Adelia was reduced to silence. She sat bolt upright on the front seat as Trish drove swiftly over the winding country roads. She was even too excited to enjoy the rolling hills and the horses grazing in the meadows, now softly outlined by the sinking afternoon sun.

Paddy was there to open the door when Adelia burst in with her new treasures.

"Little Dee, you're looking as happy as the first time you rode Majesty round the track," he said, observing her flushed, happy face.

"This was nearly as exciting, Uncle Paddy." She laughed and stepped through the doorway. "Never have I seen so many clothes, so many people. Do you know, I think everyone in America is in a constant hurry, driving, rushing through the stores—nothing ever seems to move slowly. This place Trish took me was amazing—all these shops in one big building, and it had fountains, right inside." She sighed, then shrugged and grinned. "I know I should be ashamed for squandering money the way I did, but I'm not. I had a fine time."

"It was due time, lass, due time." He kissed her cheek as they entered the living room.

"Well, Paddy, she's lost her innocence." Travis rose from an armchair and grinned down at Adelia and her packages. "Trish corrupted her. I knew I shouldn't have let that sister of mine get hold of her."

"Your sister is a wonderful lady, Mr. Grant." Adelia tossed back her head to meet his eyes, chestnut curls falling back from her face. "She has a sweet and generous soul, and a good deal more in the way of manners than some I could name."

His brow lifted, and he glanced over her head to look at Paddy as the older man struggled not to grin. "It appears Trish has a champion, and one I don't think I care to challenge." He shifted his gaze back to Adelia's irate face. "At least," he added with a slow, enigmatic smile, "not today. . . ."

Chapter Four

Saturday dawned sunny and unseasonably warm. The trees were now in full leaf, and the air carried the sweet scent of flowers as spring approached midterm. Adelia sang happily as she groomed Fortune, a sturdy three-year-old colt who listened with approval to her high, lilting voice as she brushed him.

"Dee! Dee!" She whirled around to see Mark and Mike scurrying into the stables. "Mom said we could come down and see you, and the new foal too."

"Good day to you, gentlemen; it's pleased I am to have you visiting me."

"Will you show us the foal?" Mike demanded, and she smiled at his enthusiasm.

"That I will, Master Michael, as soon as I've finished with my friend here. Now." She set down the brush and reached a hand into her back pocket. "Where is it that I put that hoof pick?" Her pockets were empty, and she searched the ground, frowning. "It's the little people at work again."

"We didn't take it," Mark objected.

"People are always blaming kids for everything," Mike complained righteously.

"Oh, but it's not children I'm speaking of," Adelia corrected. "It's leprechauns."

"Leprechauns?" the twins chorused. "What's a leprechaun?"

"Could it be you're telling me you've never heard of leprechauns?" She asked in amazement. The boys shook their identical heads, and she folded her arms across her chest. "Well, your education's sadly lacking, lads. It's a sorry thing to remain ignorant of the little people."

"Tell us, Dee," they demanded, pulling at her hands in excitement.

"That I will." She hauled herself up to sit on a bench as the two boys squatted on the floor at her feet. "Now, the leprechaun is a strange fellow, his father being an evil spirit and his mother a fairy fallen from grace. By nature he's a mischief-maker. He only grows to be about three feet high, no matter how old he happens to be. Some say he likes to be riding on sheep or goats, so a man knows, if his stock is tired and weary of a morning, that the little people have been up to their tricks and using them for some errand where they didn't want to travel on foot. They can be lazy when they've a mind to.

"They love to be making mischief about the house

as well. Why, a leprechaun'll make a pot boil over on the stove, or keep it from boiling at all, as his whim suits him. Or he'll steal the bacon or toss the furniture about for the sheer love of the confusion. Other times he'll drink his fill of the milk or poteen and fill up the bottle with water.

"Now," she continued, her eyes bright with excitement as the two boys clung to her words, "to catch a leprechaun would bring certain fortune to the one who had the wit to hold him. The only time you can catch him is when he's sitting down, and he never sits unless his brogues want mending. He's forever running about so that he wears them out, and when he feels his feet on the ground, he sits behind a hedge or in the tall grass of a meadow and takes them off to mend them. Then"——she lowered her voice to a dramatic whisper, and the two heads inched forward——"you creep up, quiet as a cat, and grab him tight in your arms." She flung her arms around an imaginary leprechaun and shouted, " 'Give me your gold,' you say. 'I've got no gold,' says he."

Releasing her invisible captive, she gave the boys a roguish smile. "Now, there's gold by the ton, and that's the truth of it, and he can tell you where it's to be found, but he won't till you make him. Now, some try choking him or threatening him, but, whatever you do, you mustn't for a moment take your eyes from him. If you do that, he's gone in a flash, and you'll not be seeing him again. The scheming devil has a pocketful of tricks for getting away, and he can charm the birds from the trees if he's a mind to. But if you hold your ground and keep your eye on him, his gold is yours, and your fortune's made."

"Did you ever see a leprechaun, Dee?" Mark asked, bouncing with excitement.

"By the saints, I thought I did, a time or two." She nodded sagely. "But I never got close enough before they had vanished, quick as you please. So"—she jumped from the bench and tousled two dark heads—"unless I'm finding me one who's traveled to America, I'll have to be working for my living." She picked up a hoof pick from the bench. "And that's what I'm doing now, or I'll be fired for laziness and be begging for pennies."

"We wouldn't let it come to that, would we, boys?"

Adelia spun around, her color rising as she met Travis's mocking smile. The thumping in her heart she attributed to surprise, and she was forced to swallow nervously before speaking.

"It's a habit you're making of creeping up on a body and frightening the wits from them, Mr. Grant."

"Maybe I mistook you for a leprechaun, Dee." His grin was annoying, but she refused to be baited and bent to lift Fortune's hoof.

He led the twins down to visit the new foal, and she set down the horse's leg and watched his broad back retreat down the passage.

Why did he always send her into a flutter? She wondered. Why did her pulses begin to race at a speed that rivaled Majesty's whenever she looked up and met those surprisingly blue eyes? She leaned her cheek against Fortune's sturdy neck and sighed. She'd lost, she conceded. She'd lost the battle, and though she fought against it, she was in love with Travis Grant. It was impossible, she admitted. Nothing could ever develop between the owner of Royal Meadows and an insignificant stablehand.

"Besides," she whispered to the understanding colt, "he's an arrogant brute of a man, and I don't believe I like him one little bit." Hearing the boys approach, she bent quickly and lifted another hoof for cleaning.

"Run along outside, boys. I want a word with Dee." At Travis's command, the twins scrambled past, chattering and exclaiming over the foal. She set down the horse's leg and straightened to face him, the color fading from her cheeks.

Blast my cursed tongue, she thought in desperate condemnation. Aunt Lettie told me a thousand times where my temper would take me.

"I—have I done something wrong, Mr. Grant?" She stammered slightly and bit her lip in frustration.

"No, Dee," he answered, slowly searching her troubled face. "Did you think I was going to fire you?" His voice was oddly gentle, and she felt a tremor at the unfamiliar tone.

"You did say I could have a fortnight, and I've a few days left before—"

"There's no need for a trial," he interrupted. "I've already decided to keep you on."

"Oh, thank you, Mr. Grant," she began, overcome with relief. "I'm grateful to you."

"Your way with horses is quite phenomenal, a strange sort of empathy." He stroked Fortune's flank, then fixed his eyes on her again. "It would be impossible to complain about your work, except that there's too much of it. I don't want to hear about you cleaning tack at ten o'clock at night anymore."

"Oh, well . . ." Turning back to the bench, Adelia gave intense concentration to placing the hoof pick in its proper spot. "I just—"

"Don't argue, and don't do it again," he commanded, and she felt his hands descend to her shoulders. "You know, you seem to split your time between working and arguing. We'll have to see if we can find another outlet for all that energy."

"I don't argue, exactly. Well, perhaps sometimes." She shrugged and wished she had the courage to turn and face him. The decision was taken out of her hands as she found herself being turned, then lifted until she once again sat on the bench.

"Perhaps sometimes," Travis agreed, and she found it disconcerting that his smile was so close, his hands still circling her waist.

"Mr. Grant," she began, then swallowed as he reached up to pluck her cap from her hair, freeing the rich cloud of auburn. "Mr. Grant, I've work to do."

"Mmm." His comment was absent as he became involved with the winding of curls around his fingers. "I've always had a fondness for chestnuts." Grinning, he gave her hair a firm tug until her face lifted to his. "A very particular fondness."

"Would you like to check my teeth?" Seeking a defense against a swift wave of longing, Adelia stiffened and sent him what she hoped was a lethal glare. His burst of unrestrained laughter caused the glare to light with green fire, and she struggled to slide from the bench.

"Oh, no." He held her still with minimum effort. "You should realize by now that I find it impossible to restrain myself when you start spitting fire."

He took her mouth quickly, one hand still tangled in her hair, the other slipping under her shirt to claim the smooth skin of her back. She found her second trip through the storm no less devastating than the first, and while her will melted under its force, her senses sharpened. The scent of leather, horses, and masculinity rose and surrounded her, a strange, intoxicating scent she knew she would always associate with him. She could feel his strength as he plunged her deeper into the kiss, demanding every drop of sweetness from her mouth. Hard and seeking, his lips parted hers, his tongue teasing hers into mobility until she was pliant and yielding against him.

For the first time she felt the pain and demand of womanhood, the slow ache growing in the center of her being and spreading to encompass her entirely, until there was nothing but the need and the man who could assuage it. She heard a soft moan as her lips were freed, not aware it was her own weak protest at liberation, and her lids opened slowly to reveal eyes dark and slumberous with desire.

"I find," Travis commented in a low, lazy voice, "that is a more productive use of time than arguing."

Adelia watched his eyes drop to the lips still warm from his and felt his hand tighten on her hair. It relaxed slowly, and a smile moved across his face as his eyes rose to hers. "It also appears to be the only way to shut you up for any amount of time."

He dropped her cap back on her head, then traced her cheek with his finger. "I find Irish tempers have definite advantages."

He strode away, and Adelia contemplated his long, graceful stride in confusion, reaching up one hand to press the cheek his finger had touched.

Pushing away a puzzle she could not solve, she spent the rest of the day in a state of euphoria. She was staying. She had found her place on the mammoth horse farm, and an uncle who wanted as well as needed her, and a job that was a dream realized. And at least, she thought happily, she would be close to Travis, seeing him almost daily, feeding her need on the sight of his tall, powerful form, on a few snatched words of conversation. That was enough for the present, and the future was something to be faced when it arrived. . . .

Long after her uncle had retired, Adelia remained wide awake. She had tried to relax with a book, but her spirits were too high for sitting idly, and she closed it and slipped outside.

She decided to walk to the stables, promising herself she would not touch one bridle but merely look in on the horses. The night remained warm, the sky blanketed with stars, so clear and vivid that she reached up, imagining she could pluck one from the soft, black curtain. At peace with the world, she meandered toward the large white building.

Entering, she switched on a low light to dispel the unrelieved darkness. She had gone no more than twenty feet when a soft moaning sound caught her attention, and she whirled in the direction of an empty stall. A man lay in a crumpled heap, and she caught her breath in alarm.

"Merciful heavens!" She hurried in and bent over him. "What's happened? Oh!" she uttered in disgust and stood, hands on hips. "You are drunk, George Johnson, and a pitiful sight indeed. You smell like a poteen factory. What do you mean drinking yourself into such a state and lying about in the stables?"

"So, it's pretty little Dee," George mumbled thickly, hauling himself into a half-sitting position. "Did you come for a visit? Come to share my bottle?"

Adelia had found herself avoiding the groom. She had often found his eyes on her, and his leering smile had caused her to recoil instinctively. Now, however, she was angry and disgusted, and she took no pains to hide it.

"No, I'll not be sharing a bottle with the likes of you—I've no patience for drunken sods. Haul yourself up and be on your way. You've no business in here with your mind fuddled with whiskey."

"Giving orders now, little Dee?" He struggled to his feet and faced her. "Too good to drink with me?" He raked her from head to foot with bleary eyes, pausing on the swell of her breast and moistening his lips. "Maybe you don't want to drink when there's more interesting things to do." He grabbed her shoulders and closed his mouth over hers, the strong smell of whiskey assaulting her senses as she pushed against him.

"You filthy pig of a man!" she spat, infuriated that he had touched her. "You great, sniveling, drunken buzzard, don't you ever put your hands on me again. You guzzling serpent, I'll kick you into next week if you touch me again." She ranted at him until he grabbed her with such force that her breath caught in her throat.

"I'll do more than touch you." His hand clamped over her mouth, and he pushed her down roughly in the straw-filled stall. She fought in wild fury, kicking and scratching as his hands began to bruise her body, choking back the sickness that rose as his lips violated hers. Her blouse ripped away from the shoulder, the sound exploding in her ear. Anger gave way to terror, and she struggled more violently. Her nails dug into his arms, tearing his skin, and as he cursed with pain and raised his head, her scream pierced the still night.

A hand slapped hard across her cheek, numbing her face as he closed his palm over her mouth again. She continued to thrash out as his free hand captured her breast and moved over her with cruel purpose. Her strength was ebbing, and she realized she was helpless against the violation that was to come. He was tugging at her jeans, his drunkenness causing his fingers to fumble at the snap. The hand over her mouth was depriving her of air, and a foggy dimness floated in front of her eyes.

Please, somebody, help me, she prayed desperately as nausea swamped her. Suddenly, she was

released from his crushing weight. She heard a
muffled curse and the soft thud of flesh on flesh.
Crawling to the stall's opening, she breathed deep to
force back the queasiness. *Travis*, she thought
dizzily, as she made out his powerful figure in the
dimly lit stable.

He was beating the smaller man with a ruthless
determination, knocking him to the floor with
crushing blows, only to drag him up again by the
shirtfront and send him sprawling once more.
George offered no resistance; indeed he could not,
she realized as her mind cleared, he was already
unconscious. Still, Travis's fist pounded, pulling the
man up on his watery legs again and again. He's
killing him, she thought suddenly, and sprang to
her feet, running toward them.

"No, Travis, you're killing him!" She grabbed the
hard, muscular arm. "For the love of God, Travis—
you're killing him!"

He jerked back, and for a moment she feared he
would brush her off like a fly and finish the man who
now lay in a motionless heap on the stable floor. As
he turned to face her, Adelia stepped away, frightened by his expression of rage. His face seemed to be
carved from granite, his eyes steely blue and pene-
trating as he stared at her. She trembled at the
strong, harsh mask and offered up a silent prayer
that she would never have that deadly fury directed
at her.

"Are you all right?" His voice was clipped, his
eyes boring into hers.

"Aye." She swallowed convulsively, dropping her

eyes from his stare. "Oh, Travis, your hands!" Without thought, she took them in her own. "They're bleeding; you'll have to tend to them. I have some salve that's—"

"Damn it, Dee." He yanked his hands away from hers, taking her by the shoulders and tilting her head back so her eyes once more met the icy fury in his. He surveyed the torn blouse, the bruises already in evidence on the creamy skin, the rich hair tousled around her pale face. "How badly did he hurt you?" His voice was low and uneven.

Dee struggled to keep her own voice calm and not give way to the hysteria bubbling below the surface. "Not badly—he just frightened me. He only hit me once." His face suffused with color, dark and angry at her words, his hands tightening uncontrollably on her shoulders. "Is he alive?" she asked, her voice barely audible. Travis he let out a long breath, released her, and turned to study the crumpled form.

"Yes, more's the pity. Heaven knows he wouldn't have been if you hadn't intervened. The police will see to him now."

"No!" Her cry of protest brought Travis's attention back to her.

"Adelia . . ." he began slowly. "The man tried to rape you, don't you understand?"

"I know very well what his intentions were." She hugged herself to control the spasmodic trembling assailing her. "But we can't call the police." She rushed on as Travis made to protest. "I don't want Uncle Paddy to know about this. I won't have him worrying and upset because of me. I'm not hurt, and I won't have Uncle Paddy upset—I tell you, I won't!" Her voice rose, and he slipped a gentle arm around her shoulders.

"All right, Dee, all right," he soothed, tightening his grip around her shuddering. "I'll call a couple of men and have him taken off the property. No police." He began to lead her from the stables. "Come on, I'll take you home."

The room began to lurch sickeningly as a roaring sound filled her brain, the dim light ebbing until she could barely see. "Travis." Her voice sounded strange and far away over the deafening roar in her head. "I'm sorry, but I'm going to faint." As she spoke, the darkness closed in and swallowed her.

Adelia opened her eyes slowly, experimentally. There was something cool and wonderful on her forehead, and someone was stroking her cheek and speaking her name. She sighed and closed her eyes again, enjoying the new sensation of pampering, before opening them once more to focus on her surroundings.

The room was lit with a warm glow, the walls a cool, soft ivory trimmed with carved dark wood. She made out a wingbacked chair and a dark mahogany table on which stood an antique globed lamp that softly lit the room. Her eyes traveled over to the man who knelt beside her and rested on Travis's face.

"I'm in the main house," she stated matter-of-factly, and his expression of concern was transformed into an amused smile.

"Leave it to you not to say the usual 'Where am I?'" He removed the wet cloth from her head and sat down beside her on the long sofa. "I don't know anyone else who could calmly announce she was sorry, she was going to faint, and then proceed to do so."

"I've never fainted before in my life," she told him, mystified. "I'm sure I don't like it."

"Well, your color's better now. I've never seen anyone go so white. You scared the daylights out of me."

"I'm sorry." She gave him a weak smile and sat up. "It was a foolish thing to do, and—" She stopped suddenly as her hand went to her throat, only to find the cross that always hung there missing. "My cross," she stammered, looking down to where her hand rested. "I must have lost it in the stables. I've got to go find it." He pushed her back firmly as she attempted to rise.

"You're in no shape to go out there now, Dee," he began, but she cut him off, struggling against his hold.

"I've got to find it. It can't be gone." Her color had drained again, and he pushed her back on the sofa.

"Dee, for heaven's sake, you'll fall flat on your face."

"Let me go. I can't lose it."

He tried to keep his words soothing, feeling helpless against her rising hysteria. He had seen her flaming angry and deeply moved, but never incoherently desperate, and he struggled to hold both her and his own temper in check. "Dee," he said shortly, giving her a small shake. "Get a grip on yourself. It's just a cross."

"It was my mother's. I've got to have it—it's all I have left of her. It's all I have." She was trembling violently, and he drew her into the warm circle of his arms and began the ageless comfort of rocking.

"I'll find it for you, don't worry. I'll go back and find it tonight."

Resting against his strong shoulder, she felt strangely content, and both panic and the threatened tears dissolved. "Do you promise?"

"Yes, Dee, I promise." He rubbed his cheek against the silk curtain of her hair, and she wondered suddenly what it was about a man that made it so good to be held by one—or was it just one man? Sighing, she allowed herself another moment's luxury pressed against him.

"I'm all right now, Mr. Grant." She drew herself away as far as his arms would permit. "I'm sorry I acted like that."

"You don't have to be sorry, Dee." His hand lifted to brush back the full, thick waves that tumbled around her face. "And it was Travis before; let's leave it at that. I rather like the way you say it."

She felt her pulses respond to his soft words and gentle touch, her awareness of him growing until she thought her veins would burst from the pressure.

"I—Is it that you're implying I have an accent?" Her brows lifted in mock censure as a defense against the suddenly dangerous atmosphere.

"No. I'm the one with the accent."

His smile drew one of her own, but the innocent

intimacy only heightened her confusion, and she felt her color rise in an unaccustomed blush, her lashes sweeping down like fragile shutters. He grinned at the uncharacteristic shyness before he rose and moved to a small bar across the room.

"I think you could use a drink before I take you home." He lifted a crystal decanter. "Some brandy?"

"Brandy's a stranger to me, but perhaps if you've some Irish . . ." She sat up straighter, grateful for the distance between them.

"I'd be hard pressed not to with Paddy as my trainer," he commented, pouring a small measure of whiskey into a glass. "Here." He walked back to her and offered the glass. "This should steady you and keep you from falling into my arms again."

She took the glass and downed its contents without a shudder as Travis watched with uplifted brows. He looked down at the empty glass she handed him before bursting into gales of laughter.

"And what would you be finding so funny?" Tilting her head, she regarded him with curious eyes.

"That a half-pint like you could down two fingers of whiskey as though it were a cup of tea."

"Aye, well, it comes with the blood, I suppose. I'm not one that drinks often, but when I do I can handle my liquor—which is more than can be said of that slimy pig of a groom." He turned back to set the empty glass on the bar so that she was unaware of the hardening of his features. "Travis . . ." she said, hesitating over his name, and he turned, relaxing his face into calm lines. "I'm grateful to you for what you did." Standing, she moved until she stood in front of him. "I'm owing you, Travis, though God Himself knows how I'll ever repay you."

His eyes were intense for a moment, brooding over the face she turned up to his; then his features relaxed into a smile, and he ran his finger down her cheek. "Perhaps one day I'll call in the debt."

The sun streamed onto the kitchen table as Adelia removed the postbreakfast clutter. She was grateful Paddy had noticed nothing amiss, having been fast asleep when, late and disheveled, she had arrived back home. He had greeted her that morning with his usual cheery smile, and she had mirrored it, firmly blocking the memory of her night's encounter from her mind. Hearing footsteps approach the kitchen, she closed the door on the dishwasher.

"I'm just coming, Uncle Paddy. I've got the buttons all figured out now. It's amazing how— Oh!" She stopped as she turned and saw Travis leaning against the doorway. "Good morning." She pushed at her hair as her thought processes skidded to a halt.

"How are you?" He walked toward her, eyes traveling in an intense survey.

"I'm f-fine, just f-fine," she stammered, and despised herself. Will I always behave like this when he comes on me unexpectedly? she demanded of herself, and determinedly offered a slight smile. His hand cupped her chin, and Adelia held very still as he searched her face.

"Are you sure?"

She nodded; then, realizing she had been holding her breath, she let it out slowly. "I'm fine, really."

Her eyes traveled past him, and he read her concern easily.

"Paddy's already gone. I told him I needed to speak with you for a minute." Releasing her chin, Travis reached into his pocket and pulled out her cross and chain.

"Oh, you found it!" Her face lifted to his, illuminating the room more brilliantly than the sun. "Thank you, Travis, for troubling. It means a great deal to me."

"There's no need to thank me, Dee, and it wasn't a question of troubling." He tucked a strand of hair behind her ear in a gentle gesture that threatened to dissolve her knees. "The clasp is broken. I'll have it repaired for you."

"You don't have to do that. I can—"

"I said I'll have it repaired." His voice was firm, and her brows drew together at the underlying anger in his tone. Letting out a long breath, he slipped the cross back into his pocket, then carefully framed her face with his hands. "Adelia, I'm responsible for what happened last night. No, don't argue," he commanded as her mouth opened to contradict. "What happens to you—to the people who work for me—" he amended, "is my responsibility. I wanted you to know I'd found your cross, so you wouldn't worry. I'll have the chain repaired and get it back to you as soon as possible."

"All right," she murmured, finding currents of pleasure brushing along her skin as his hands continued to cup her face as if it were something fragile and precious.

He smiled, and his thumb traced her lips with a

teasing lightness. "At times, Dee, you can be surprisingly docile. Then, just when I think you've been halter broke, you start bucking again."

Drawing away, Adelia straightened her shoulders. "I'm not a mare to be pulled about on a lead line."

Smile became grin. Travis tousled her hair before taking her hand and pulling her from the room. "Maybe you'll find it depends who's holding the line."

The days passed slowly for Adelia as the two main men in her life were absent for a time. Paddy had accompanied Majesty to Florida in preparation for the Flamingo Stakes. She found, for one who had always taken her own self-sufficiency for granted, that the nights grew longer without Paddy's company. The house seemed large and quiet and empty. Alone in the evening, she reflected how easily a heart could be lost to another. In less time than it takes for the moon to go from full glory to a sliver of light, love had swept over her, leaving her vulnerable. Love for Paddy, a sweet, full warmth of belonging, and love for Travis, an aching, spreading need.

She built a fire, though the spring air was kind through opened windows, and curled up in front of its company, her head resting on the arm of her chair. Paddy would be home the next day, and she found the knowledge comforting, for with his presence there would not be so many hours alone, so many hours to think. Travis would not leave her thoughts or her heart, and seeing him daily brought as much torment as it did delight.

As the fire grew soft and low in the grate, her mind drifted to him, her lashes fluttering down to conceal her dreams, her hair falling in a curtain against her cheek.

"Dee." She stirred in the twilight world of dreams, sighing as a hand brushed through her hair. "Dee, wake up."

Lids opened slowly, and eyes misted with sleep focused on Travis. Her hand lifted to touch his cheek before fantasy was completely dimmed. "Oh." Dropping her hand, she struggled to sit up, pushing back her hair to look up at him. "Travis." She felt fresh color warm her sleep-flushed cheeks and pulled the neck of her faded blue robe closer together. "I must have fallen asleep."

"If I could have understood how anyone could be comfortable in that position, I would have left you alone." Smiling, he moved from his crouched position to sit on the arm where her cheek had rested.

Desperately aware of his nearness, Adelia pushed far into the corner of the chair, her hands clasped in her lap. "I was just thinking that Uncle Paddy would be home tomorrow," she said with partial honesty.

"Yes. I'd like to have gone with him, but I just couldn't get away." He laid a finger under her chin and lifted it. The dying power of the fire danced in her hair. "You've missed him."

"Aye." Her smile spread as her eyes traveled over his face. "And Majesty as well." His smile answered hers, and as the moment grew long, she felt the need to abort the contact. "I'm sorry Majesty didn't win his race." Her fingers smoothed the skirts of her robe.

"Hmm?" His hands were exploring the flickers of light in her hair, and she repeated her statement in a rush of words.

"Oh well, he placed and made a good run. Winning takes time, Dee." With a laugh, Travis ruffled her hair. "Time, patience, and strategy. . . . Look, I have something for you." Reaching into his pocket, he drew out her cross. "I didn't have the opportunity to give it to you earlier today."

"Oh, Travis, thank you." She lifted her face again to smile. "It means a great deal."

"I know." Instead of handing it to her, Travis opened the clasp and slipped the chain around her neck. His fingers on her skin were warm and gentle, and Adelia lowered her eyes, struggling not to tremble. "Better?" he asked when the clasp was secured, and she nodded, swallowing before the words would come.

"Much better, thank you, Travis."

He studied her bent head a moment; then, taking her hand, he pulled her to her feet. "Come on, close the door behind me and go to bed. You're tired." Reaching the door, he paused, one hand on the knob. "You look like a child." Her chestnut hair hung loose and heavy over the shoulders of her robe, and he ran a hand down the length of it. "A child can't be bundled off to bed without a goodnight kiss," he said softly. Before she could step away, his hand had circled her neck, his mouth lowering to linger on her cheek while her lips parted in hunger. Her hunger was to go unsatisfied, for his mouth barely brushed her other cheek. As in a dream, she watched him straighten, then turn to leave, closing the door gently behind him. . . .

With Paddy's return Royal Meadows threw itself into preparing Majesty for the Bluegrass Stakes. The race was a preliminary for the most prestigious race in the country, the Kentucky Derby. Majesty's record was impressive, and his good showing in Florida had hopes running high for his next venture on the track.

Adelia leaned on the fence surrounding the track, chin resting on crossed arms, as Steve Parker, the young jockey, raced Majesty around the large oval. There had been an immediate liking between her and the small man, an easy rapport born of a mutual love of horses. She watched their progress around the track, enjoying their fluid harmony.

Pushing the button on the stopwatch he was holding, Paddy let out a loud whoop of approval before he handed it to Travis. "If he runs like that in Kentucky, there's not another horse will come within five lengths of him at the finish. He holds the turns like a lover."

"Aye, and he runs for the sheer love of it," Adelia murmured, sighing as Steve brought the colt toward them in a slow walk.

"Let's hope he loves it as much in Kentucky," Travis put in and sauntered over to speak to his jockey.

"Are you excited about your first race, little Dee?" Paddy asked, ruffling her hair.

"You might say I'm a bit excited," she returned

with a grin. "My eyes will be glued to the television; not even a ton of dynamite could blast me away."

"Television?" Paddy repeated, the skin crinkling around his eyes as he narrowed them. "What's put it in your mind about television? You'll be coming with us."

"Coming with you?" She stared back in confusion.

"Of course, Adelia." She spun around at Travis's voice, her eyes making contact with his hard chest before she tilted her head back to meet his calm, controlled gaze.

"Now why would I be doing that?"

"Because," he answered evenly, "I say so."

"Is that the way of it?" she demanded, infuriated by the tone of command in his voice. "Well, if it's a groom you need, there's others who've been here longer. Stan or Tom deserves to go more than me."

"But, Dee," Steve protested with a wide grin as he joined them, "you're much prettier than those two. I'd rather look at you—you'll give me inspiration."

"Inspiration, is it?" she returned, amused by the compliment. "You're mad as a hatter." She turned to Travis again, shifting her eye level by several long inches. "I think you'd best take one of the men," she began, but he cut her off, narrowing his eyes and grabbing her hand.

"Excuse us," he called over his shoulder as he began to stride off, dragging Adelia in his wake. When at last he stopped some distance away, she rounded on him furiously.

"What the devil do you mean racing off like that

and carting me behind you?" she panted, outraged.
"Your legs are almost as long as my whole body, and
I had to fair run to keep up with you."

She glared up at him, a picture of righteous
indignation.

"I prefer to argue in private, Adelia," Travis said
coolly, meeting her mutinous face with nonchalant
command. "I run Royal Meadows and I give the
orders." Even through her own anger, Adelia could
see the signs of temper held in check; his eyes hard
and direct, he was suddenly the essence of the
master. "I will not have you countermanding my
orders privately, and most certainly not publicly."
His words annoyed her further simply because she
knew he was right. "You're going to have to get it
through that stubborn head of yours that you are no
longer in solitary control of what is to be done. Now,
I believe the issue here is your presence in Kentucky," he went on calmly, his face expressionless.

"I was telling you—"

"I'm telling you," he interrupted imperiously.
"You're going."

Her eyes flashed at the order. Why, she thought, if
it's God's pleasure for me not to be forever bursting
with temper did He give me such a demanding one?

"Majesty responds better to you than anyone
else," Travis went on. "I want you tending to him."
Anger receded slowly at his words, and she dropped
her eyes, staring at the ground while she considered
his statement. "You'll come to Kentucky because it
suits me to have you there, and I'm accustomed to
having what suits me." His smile spread in a rapid
change of mood as her head snapped up with fresh

anger. His hands claimed her waist, then trailed slowly upward, resting on the sides of her firm young breasts as her anger faded into confusion. Lingering, his thumbs caressed in a slow circle, then trailed once in a lazy arch over the subtle curves, pausing at their fullness before moving to rest under their soft swell. Her lips parted, but she found no strength to protest against the unfamiliar intimacy, her body responding to his touch, eclipsing her will. She felt herself rising from the ground, and her hands went to his shoulders automatically to compensate for the loss of gravity.

"Put me down." The order emerged as a trembling whisper, and his smile grew wider before his mouth lowered.

"In a minute."

His mouth was dominant and sure, and her fingers dug into his shoulders as the force of the kiss held her in its prison. With a final flash of lucidity, she knew she could never fight Travis on these terms. Then all was lost in the dark demand of need.

"Steve's right," he murmured, his teeth nibbling at her lip and sending shooting sparks of flame through her veins. "You are prettier than Tom or Stan."

With a final hard, brief kiss, he dropped her back to the ground, to stride away with casual arrogance, whistling the first few bars of "My Wild Irish Rose." Adelia stood gaping after him, trembling with a confusing mixture of indignation and longing.

Chapter Five

Adelia found herself on a plane for the second time in her life. This plane, however, was vastly different from the crowded economy section of the passenger jet in which she had traveled over the Atlantic. Now she was passing over the relatively short distance between Maryland and Kentucky in the lush comfort of Travis's specially equipped private jet. Adelia's attitude during this flight was also a marked variation from her first. She stared, mesmerized, from the window, fascinated by the topography of far-distant West Virginia.

She looked down on patchworks of green and umber dotted by small houses, toy-train cities and gray ribbons of roads snaking and winding to connect them. There were rivers and pine-topped mountains, their colors soft from her eagle view, and she thought with pleasure that the world was indeed a wondrous place. Engrossed in her new discoveries, she did not notice when Travis sat next to her.

"Enjoying the view, Dee?" he asked at length, smiling at the way she pressed her forehead to the glass like a child at a bakery window. She started at his voice, then turned her head to face him, pushing back the chestnut curls that spilled over her face at the movement.

"Merciful heavens, you're forever surprising me. You move like the wind through a willow."

"Sorry. I'll practice stomping." He grinned and shifted in his seat to regard her more directly. "I've often thought you move like one of those fairies Ireland's so famous for, or maybe one of your leprechauns."

"Oh, well, it can't be both. A leprechaun's not considered a fit associate for a reputable fairy."

"Only a disreputable fairy," he returned, amused at the sobriety of her statement.

"Aye, and for the most part they're on their good behavior, hoping to be readmitted to Paradise on the last day."

"Tossed out, were they?"

"When Satan was rebelling, they stood back from the fighting, not wanting to take sides till they knew how it would end. But since that was their only offense, they were banished to earth instead of tossed into the pit with the rebels."

"Seems fair," Travis concluded with a nod. "As I recall, they have the rather awesome power to turn one into a dog or a pig or something equally undesirable, but are normally disposed to good deeds if treated with the proper respect."

"That's right," she agreed. "How did you know that?"

"Paddy saw to the holes in my education." He leaned over her, smiling, and she pressed back into the cushions, green eyes growing wide. "Relax." His voice tightened in annoyance. "I'm not going to eat you." He fastened the seat belt around her waist and leaned back. "We'll be landing in a minute."

"So soon?" She controlled her voice to casualness while the beating of her heart vibrated in her ears.

"That's right," he answered, matching her tone as he secured his own belt. "You've been staring down at Kentucky for some time now."

With amazing organization and economy of movement, the plane was landed, Majesty was unloaded and transferred to a waiting van, and the travelers were on their way to Churchill Downs.

Adelia's impression of Louisville was vague. Her mind was in the back of the van with Majesty. She worried that he might be frightened and confused by the strange sights and long transport. When she voiced her concern, she was rewarded with a deep, full laugh from Travis. The ominous gleam in her eye was ignored as, chuckling, he informed her that Majesty was a seasoned traveler and took it in his stride.

Her irritation had faded by the time the van reached the extensive stables at Churchill Downs. Travis immediately confirmed the arrangements that had been made for Majesty's stall space and feed.

Travis Grant was well known and highly respected in racing circles. Adelia noted that he was greeted with warmth by the men and women milling around the stable area. He stood head and shoulders above the group, exuding power and a virile masculinity which, she observed with a rude stab of jealousy, was obviously appreciated by the women who greeted him. Infuriated with herself for her own weakness, Adelia turned sharply back to Majesty and led the gleaming colt into his stall.

Time passed swiftly as she tended to the animal's needs, brushing and soothing as she kept up a flow of one-sided chatter. As she was completing her duties, she heard loud footsteps approaching and turned around to see who was causing the din.

"Loud enough?" Travis grinned at her with unexpected boyishness.

"Aye," she agreed and gave him a solemn nod. "You sounded like a herd of great African elephants. You're a funny man, Travis," she commented, tilting her head to the side and studying him.

"Am I, Dee? How?"

"There's times you're like the local squire tossing orders about, and the steel in your eyes could freeze a man in his tracks. Then I think you're a hard man. But then sometimes . . ." Faltering, she shrugged and turned back to Majesty.

"Don't stop now." Deliberately, he turned her back to face him, a faint smile playing on his mouth. "You've intrigued me."

She was uncomfortable now and wishing with a full heart that she would learn to think before speaking. But Travis ignored her expression of embarrassment, hands light but firm on her shoulders, eyes demanding her elaboration.

"Sometimes . . . I've seen you laughing and talking with the men, or carting one of the twins about
on your shoulders. And I see the way it is between
you and Uncle Paddy, and the way you treat your
horses. I think then maybe there's a gentle side, and
maybe you're not so hard, after all." She finished in
a rush, wishing she had never started, and turned
back to give Majesty unnecessary additional attention with the brush.

"That's very interesting," he commented, taking
the brush from her hand and continuing the grooming himself. "She's spoiling you," he addressed
Majesty, running an affectionate hand along his
flank. "She'd stand in here rubbing you down for the
next hour if I let her."

She tore her eyes from Travis's fingers as they
stroked the rich chestnut hide. "I don't spoil him; it
was just love and care I was giving. We all need that
from time to time."

He turned his head and met her eyes with a long,
level look. "Yes, we all need that from time to
time."

That night, awake in the unfamiliar hotel room,
Adelia tossed and turned, ultimately rolling over
and pounding her innocent pillow. Love was decid-
edly uncomfortable, unpredictable, and unwelcome.
Sighing, she hugged the pillow she had just beaten,
determined to erase incredibly blue eyes from her
dreams.

The next morning Adelia had her first real look at
Churchill Downs. Leading Majesty from the stables,

she stopped as she came to the track, her companion waiting with calm indulgence as she stared in open amazement.

The grounds were enormous, the wide mile-and-a-quarter track encircling a grass field bordered by fences and graced with well-shaped shrubs and flower beds of brilliant color. Moving her eyes over the vast expanse of stands, she wondered somewhat whimsically who would be left to tend to the outside world when they were filled with people. The tops of the stands were roofed, crowned with spires, she noted.

"Something wrong, Dee?" Her observations were interrupted by Travis's question, and she jumped in surprise. "Sorry," he said without bothering to conceal a grin. "Forgot to stomp."

"I should be getting used to it by now." She sighed and began to lead Majesty along once more. "What a grand place this is." Her hand swept in an expressive arch as he fell into step beside her.

"It's one of my favorites. The architecture's basically the same as it was when it was built over a hundred years ago. And, as you well know, it's the most famous track of all because it is here that the Derby is run. And the Derby, everyone remembers. On the first Saturday in May, this ribbon of track is gold, and for a few minutes the world stops, and it's only the race." He turned to her with a smile. "It all comes down to the challenge at the turn for home, when the goal is still a quarter of a mile away. Since eighteen seventy-five the best horses have run here, and the best horses have won here. It's not only the classic race, it's a breeders' race, and there isn't anyone in the States who wouldn't rather produce a winner in this than in any other contest. The winner of a Derby becomes the horse to beat for the rest of the season; the magic stays with him. And this," he continued, giving Majesty a friendly slap on the flank, "is one who likes to win."

"Aye, that he does," she agreed, giving Majesty an indulgent smile. "And he's not shy about his own capabilities. He's feeling pretty sure of himself. He wants the Bluegrass Stakes out of the way so he can move on to the Derby."

"Does he?" The corner of his mouth tilted as Majesty nuzzled Adelia's shoulder. "And how do you feel?" His finger touched her cheek, and she turned to face him. "Do you want the prep race out of the way so you can dive into the Derby?"

"I'm not ready for the first one yet." Adelia shrugged, nearly stumbling as Majesty's head nudged at her back. "It's him that's in the hurry. But I like the looks of this place." Again, she encompassed Churchill Downs with a sweep of the hand. "I like knowing it hasn't changed much in all these years." She began to walk again, at Majesty's urging. "Never did I think to see such a place."

"There are other tracks that are perhaps more eye-catching," he commented, following her fascinated gaze. "At Hialeah in Florida, they have hundreds of pink flamingos in the center-field lake."

Stopping, she turned to him with wide eyes. "I should like to see that."

"I'm sure you will," he murmured, twining his fingers in the ends of her long, silky waves. Then, pulling the brim of her cap down over her eyes, he repeated in a lighter tone, "Yes, Dee, I'm sure you will."

The week moved swiftly, hours crammed with duties and activities. Most of Adelia's time was given to Majesty's care, talking and fondling as much as grooming and seeing to his more practical needs. She spent much of her free time with Steve Parker, teasing him about his girlfriends or watching from the rail as he accustomed Majesty to the track. Other times she spent with Paddy, discussing the Thoroughbred's qualities and the style of the other colts who would compete in the qualifying race.

"The colt that wins is automatically eligible for the Derby," he informed her, giving Majesty a thorough examination as she watched from the stall door. "Of course, Travis nominated this fellow right after he was born, the same way he's entered Solomy's foal, and kept up with the nomination as he got older. He knows when he's got a winner. Travis is a man who keeps one eye on the future."

"He's good with the horses," Adelia commented. The obvious pride and affection in Paddy's voice warmed her. "You can see he cares for them; it's not just a matter of the money they'll bring him."

"Aye, he cares," Paddy agreed, giving Majesty an affectionate slap on the flank. "And he's fierce on the matter of using painkillers or drugs as others have been known to do. If one of Travis's horses isn't up for the race, he doesn't run and that's that. Of course, money's not a problem with Travis, but it wouldn't make any difference if it was, because that's the man he is. Now, he has a practical side as well." He moved from the stall to join Adelia and slipped an arm around her shoulder. "Investments—and he's mighty crafty about them. He knows how to take a purse or the sale of a foal and turn it into more. He's got the touch," Paddy added with a wise nod. "And a time or two, he's stretched my pennies for me, though not on as grand a scale as his. Travis takes care of his own." Squeezing her shoulder, Paddy led Adelia out into the flash of sunlight. She remained silent, thinking of this new aspect of the man she loved.

The sky was overcast on the day of the Bluegrass Stakes. The air was heavy. Lead-gray clouds lay thick as a blanket overhead. Tension seemed to start at Adelia's brow and spread down to her toes; the stillness of the air weighed like a stone at the nape of her neck. To take her thoughts off the coming race she kept both hands and mind busy. Glancing up she saw Travis enter the building. She smiled as he approached.

"I believe that, if you could, you'd get into the silks and ride him today."

"The truth of it is," she began, finding the ease of his smile soothing, "I think I'd be less terrified that way. But I don't think Steve would care for it."

"No." The syllable was accompanied by a slow, grave nod. "I don't think he would. Come up to the stands with me. Paddy'll take over now."

"Oh, but—" Her objection was neatly cut off as he captured her arm and propelled her to the door. "Wait!" she cried and pivoted to run swiftly back to Majesty, throwing her arms around his neck and whispering in his ear.

When she rejoined Travis, he stared down at her, both amused and frankly curious. "What did you tell him?"

She gave him a mysterious smile for an answer. As they approached the stands, she dug into her back pocket and thrust some bills into his hands. "Will you place a wager for me? I don't know how to go about it."

"A wager?" he repeated, looking down at the two dollars in his hand. Looking up, his features were entirely too serious. "Who do you want to bet on?"

"Majesty, of course." She frowned at the question, her expression lightening as she recalled some of the terms she had heard tossed around the stables. "To win . . . on the nose."

To his credit, Travis's features remained grave. "I see. Well, let's see . . . his odds are five to two at the moment." Brows drawn, he studied the odds board. "Now, number three there is ten to one, but that's not too long for a gambler. Number six is two to one; that's rather conservative."

"I don't know about all that," she interrupted with a frustrated wave of her hand. "It's just all a bunch of numbers."

"Adelia." He said her name slowly, giving her a small pat on the shoulder. "One must never bet unless one knows the odds." Ignoring her, he glanced back up at the flashing numbers. "It's three to one on number two, a nice safe choice for win, place, or show. It's eight to five on number one."

"Travis, you're making my head spin with all of this. I just want to—"

"And fifteen to one on number five." He looked

down at the two crumpled bills. "You could amass a small fortune if that one came in."

"It's not for the money." Her breath came out in one impatient huff. "It's for the luck."

"Ah, I see," he returned with a solemn nod before the grin escaped and spread. "Irish luck is not to be scoffed at."

Though she scowled quite fiercely for a moment, he slipped his arm over her shoulders and led her to the two-dollar window.

Before long, she was standing next to him and gaping openly at the masses of people filling the stands. The enormous stadium would hold one hundred and twenty-five thousand, Travis had informed her, and to her astonished eyes there seemed to be no less than that. Several people greeted Travis, and she felt an occasional twinge of discomfort as eyes often passed over her in speculation. Embarrassment was soon eclipsed by excitement as post time approached. She watched the horses step onto the track, her eyes immediately focusing on Majesty and the rider in brilliant red and gold silks on his back. As Majesty's name was announced, Adelia closed her eyes, finding the combination of excitement and nerves nearly overpowering.

"He looked ready," Travis commented casually, then laughed as she jolted at his words. "Relax, Dee, it's just another race."

"I'll never be easy about it if I see a hundred," she vowed. "Oh, here comes Uncle Paddy. Is it going to start?"

For answer, he pointed, and she watched the horses being loaded into the starting gate. Her hand clutched at the cross at her neck, and she felt Travis's arm slip over her shoulder as the bell sounded and ten powerful forms lunged forward.

It seemed to her a mass of flying hooves and thunderous noise, the pack clinging together in one speeding block. Still, her eyes were glued on Majesty as though he were racing alone. Her hand reached up of its own accord to grasp the one on her shoulder, tightening as she urged the colt to greater speed. Steadily he moved forward, as if following her remote-control command, persistently passing one, then another, until he emerged alone from the field. Suddenly the long legs increased their stride, streaking across the dirt track until his competitors were left with the sight of his massive hindquarters as he lunged under the wire.

Travis's arm encircled her, and Adelia found herself crushed to his hard chest, sandwiched between his lean body and her uncle's stocky frame. It was like being caught fast between two unmoving, loving walls, and she found the sensation tortuously wonderful, a heady mixture of scents and textures. Her uncle's voice was raised in excitement in her ear, and her head was snuggled, as if it belonged, against Travis's chest. Majesty's win, she decided, closing her eyes, was the best present she had ever had.

Every man, woman, and child in Louisville ate, slept, and breathed the Kentucky Derby. As the days dwindled, the very air seemed to shimmer with anticipation. Adelia saw Travis sporadically. Their conversations revolved around the colt, the only personal aspect of their relationship being the abstracted pat on the head he would give her from time to time. She began to think that quarreling with him had had its advantages, and she relieved her frustrations by spending more time with Majesty.

"You're a fine, great horse," she told him, holding his muzzle and looking into hi intelligent eyes. "But you mustn't let all of this go to your head. You've a job to do come Saturday, and it's a big one. Now, I'm going out for a few minutes, and I want you to rest yourself, then perhaps we'll see about a currying."

Satisfied with Majesty's silent agreement, Adelia stepped out of the stables into the bright May sun and found herself surrounded by reporters.

"Are you the groom in charge of Royal Meadows' Majesty?" The question was fired out by one of the people who suddenly cut her off from the rest of the world with a wall of bodies. The sensation was disconcerting, and she was thinking wistfully of the dim solitude of the stables when she heard another voice.

"You don't see many grooms that look like this one."

She rounded on the man who had spoken, squinting against the sun to see more clearly. "Is that the truth, now?" she demanded, discomfort replaced by annoyance. "I thought red hair was common enough in America."

The group roared with laughter, and the man at whom her remark had been directed responded with a good-natured grin. Questions were fired at her, and for a few moments she surrendered to the pressure and answered, valiantly attempting to keep one query separate from the next.

"By the saints!" She threw up her hands in dismay, shaking her head. "You're all speaking in a muddle." Pushing the brim of her cap back from her head, she took a deep breath. "If it's more information you're wanting, you'd best ask Mr. Grant or Majesty's trainer." She pushed through them with determination, turning when she felt a hand on her arm and finding herself facing the reporter who had made the personal observation.

"Miss Cunnane, sorry if we were a little rough on you." He smiled with considerable charm, and Adelia found herself smiling back.

"No harm was done."

"I'm Jack Grodon. Maybe you'd let me make it up to you by taking you out to dinner tonight."

She was both surprised and flattered by the invitation, gaining the pure feminine pleasure of having an attractive man pay her specific attention. He was, however, a stranger, and she was opening her mouth to decline when a voice sounded behind her.

"Sorry, my groom's off limits."

She whirled around to see Travis watching them, blue eyes cool and direct. Fury bubbled inside her, reflecting plainly in her flashing eyes.

"Don't you have some work to do, Adelia?" he asked with an imperial lift of brows. The eyes that met his told him without words what she thought of his question before she wheeled around and stalked to the stables.

Some fifteen minutes later, Travis disengaged himself from the avid reporters and joined her. She watched as he strode toward her, hands carelessly thrust in the pockets of slim-fitting jeans.

"Don't you know better than to make dates with strange men, Adelia?" His tone was deliberate, superior, and infuriating.

"My personal life is my own affair," she raged at him. "You've no right to interfere."

"As long as you're in my employ and responsible for my horses, your life is my affair."

"Aye, Master Grant," she tossed back, undaunted by the narrowing of his eyes. "I'll be certain to ask your permission before I take my next breath." Her foot stomped in temper. "I didn't arrive on this earth yesterday. I can take care of myself."

"Were you taking care of yourself in the stables a couple of weeks ago?" She paled at this and turned away. With a muttered curse, he turned her around to face him. "Dee, I'm sorry. That wasn't fair."

"No, it wasn't." She jerked away, eyes bright with angry tears. "But it doesn't surprise me you'd be saying it. You've a habit of putting me in my place, Master Grant, and I've been reminded there's work to be done. So be off with you and let me be about it." Removing her cap, she dropped a curtsy. "If it please Your Honor."

"I've had just about enough, you green-eyed witch," he muttered, taking a step toward her. "I'd like to haul you over my knee for the spanking you deserve, but I'll get more out of this sort of punishment."

He had her crushed against him with a speed that

allowed her only a short gasp of protest before his mouth descended, hard, then demanding, then possessing, in rapid succession. When he lifted his mouth, she felt him drawing her soul through her eyes.

"I'm not going to make a habit of this," he muttered and took her lips again, his fingers tangling in her hair, then moving over her back until she thought she would perish from the heat.

Feather-light tremors followed the trail of his hand along her spine, touching her with an exquisite fear. She felt the pressure of his arms bending her back, his mouth hard on hers, demanding not response but submission. She became aware of her own slightness, a fragility she had never known was part of her, as his strength overpowered even the thought of struggle. Lucidity drifted from her, leaving only the feel of a hard body and a demanding mouth which took from her until even to breathe was impossible.

Drawing away, Travis held Dee steady as she staggered. He stood a moment looking down thoughtfully into her flushed face. "You know, Dee," he said at length, his voice as calm and unperturbed as she was ruffled and confused, "you're too little to possess such a dangerous temper."

Flicking a friendly finger down her nose, he strode out into the sunshine.

 - The day of the Derby was an advertisement for spring, warm with a soft, scented breeze under a clear, cloudless sky. The perfection of the weather meant nothing to Adelia, whose nerves were so tightly coiled that it could have easily been midwinter. Seeing Travis several times during the morning and early afternoon, she was both envious and annoyed by his calm, easygoing manner while she remained a massive bundle of quivering nerves. Between the lingering sensation of her last encounter with him and the prospect of the race, she found functioning at even borderline normality an effort. Waiting through the preliminary races was sheer torture.

She found herself beside Travis in the stands, thinking that if the race did not begin soon she would have to be carted away and locked up until it was over.

"Here." Adelia glanced down at the glass he offered before raising her eyes to his.

"What is it?"

"A mint julep." Taking her hand, he placed the glass in it and curled her fingers around it. "Drink it," he commanded, then smiled at the frown she gave it. "The purpose is twofold. One, it's traditional, and you can keep the glass to remember your first Derby. And two," he continued, grinning, "you need something to calm your nerves; I'm afraid you're going to keel over."

"So am I," she admitted and sipped gingerly from the glass. "Travis, I would swear there are more people here than the last time. Where do they all come from?"

"Everywhere," he returned easily, following her fascinated gaze. "The Run for the Roses is the most important race of the season."

"Why do they call it that?" she asked, finding the

combination of conversation and mint julep soothing.

"The winner's draped with a blanket of red roses
in the Winner's Circle, and the jockey gets an
armful. So," he concluded and lifted his own glass,
"it's the Run for the Roses."

"That's nice," she approved, lifting the brim of
her cap further on her head. "Majesty will like red
roses."

"I'm sure he'll be crazy about them," Travis
agreed with suspicious sobriety, and Adelia's digni-
fied retort was interrupted by the first strains of "My
Old Kentucky Home."

"Oh, Travis, the parade's starting!" She fastened
her eyes on Majesty and the small man on his back,
clad in colorful red and gold silks. The others with
their brilliant contrasts of blues and greens and
yellows paled before her eyes. To her there was not
another animal to compare in power and beauty with
Travis's Thoroughbred colt—and, judging by the
way Majesty pranced, he agreed completely.

"Saints preserve us, Uncle Paddy," she murmured
as he appeared at her side. "My heart's pounding so
I'm sure it'll burst. I don't think I'm made for this."

Her eyes never left Majesty's form as he was
loaded into the gate. Her senses swam with the blare
of the trumpets and the roar of the crowd. With a
swiftness that took her breath away, the doors were
released and the horses sprang forward in a turbulent herd.

Her eyes followed the colt as he galloped with
steady assurance around the track. She was not even

aware that as the bell had rung she had grabbed Travis's hand in a viselike grip, squeezing tighter as each heart-pounding second passed. The air shivered with the voice of the crowd, individual calls and shouts melding into one trembling roar. She rode every inch of the track on Majesty's back, feeling the rush of wind on her face and the strong rhythm of the colt's gait under her.

As they rounded the second turn, Steve brought Majesty to the inside rail, and the colt took his head and left the field with long, smooth strides. The gap between the chestnut and his nearest competitor widened with what appeared to be effortless ease as he streaked down the back stretch into the home stretch and under the wire more than four lengths in the lead.

Without hesitation, Adelia threw herself into Travis's arms, clinging with a joy which she could only express physically by babbling incoherent and self-interrupted sentences to both him and her uncle, who was improvising an enthusiastic jig beside her.

"Come on." Travis tossed an arm around Paddy's shoulders. "We've got to get down to the Winner's Circle before the crowd's too thick."

"I'll wait for you." Adelia pulled back, stooping to retrieve her dislodged cap. "I don't like all those reporters staring and snapping and jumping all over me with their questions. I'll wait on the outside and take Majesty along when it's over."

"All right," Travis agreed. "But tonight, we celebrate. What do you say, Paddy?"

"I say I've just acquired a strong yearning for champagne." The two men grinned at each other.

That evening, Adelia stared at the reflection in the full-length mirror of her room. Her hair lay full and lush on her shoulders, shining like newly minted copper against the muted greens of her dress.

"Well, Adelia Cunnane, look at you." She smiled with satisfaction into the mirror. "There's not a one back in Skibbereen who'd be knowing you in such a dress, and that's the truth of it." A knock sounded at her door, and she plucked her key from the dresser. "I'm coming, Uncle Paddy."

Opening the door with a dazzling smile, she was not greeted by her merry-faced uncle but by an incredibly attractive Travis in a dark dinner suit, the white silk of his shirt startling against his deep tan. They stood silently for a moment as his gaze roamed over her, from shining hair and deep green eyes to the soft, rounded curves outlined by the clinging jersey. His gaze rose to her face again, but still he did not smile.

"Well, Adelia, you're astonishingly beautiful."

Her eyes widened at the compliment, and she searched for something suitable to say. "Thank you," she finally managed. "I thought you'd be Uncle Paddy."

His eyes continued to hold her in the doorway, and she moistened her lips with the tip of her tongue in an innocently inviting gesture. "Paddy's meeting us downstairs with Steve."

The single-minded intensity with which she was being studied was rapidly stripping her of all composure, and her words tumbled out quickly. "We'd best be joining them—they'll be waiting."

Travis merely nodded, a slight inclination of his head, and she took a step toward him, only to stop nervously when he made no move to let her pass. Raising her eyes from his shirtfront to his face, she opened her mouth to speak, only to find her mind a vacuum. He gazed down at her for another unnerving moment, then held up a single red rose, placing it in her hand.

"Majesty sent it. He says you're fond of red roses."

"Oh." He was not smiling with the whimsy of his words, and her mind fidgeted for something to ease the sudden awareness, the physical strength of his gaze. "I didn't know you talked to horses."

"I'm learning," he answered simply, and ran a finger over her bare shoulder. "My teacher's an expert."

She dropped her eyes to the bloom in her hand, thinking that twice in her life she had been given flowers, and both times they had come from Travis, both times they had been red roses. She smiled, knowing she would never again see a red rose without thinking of him. That was a gift more precious than jewels. Open and innocent, her smile lifted for him.

"Thank you, Travis, for bringing it to me." On impulse, she rose to her toes and kissed his cheek.

He stared down at her, and for a moment Adelia thought she saw some hesitation, some indecision, flicker in his eyes before his features relaxed into a smile.

"You're welcome, Dee. Bring it along—it suits you." Taking the key from her hand, he placed it in his pocket and led her to the elevator.

The celebration dinner was a new experience for Adelia. The elegant restaurant, the unaccustomed dishes, and her first encounter with champagne combined to give her a glowing sense of unreality. The tension brought on by the few moments alone with Travis was dispelled by his casually friendly attitude during the meal. It was almost as though the awareness that had passed between them had never taken place. The evening drifted by in a haze of happiness.

The following week, however, found her back in Maryland in jeans and cap, busily fulfilling her duties and thrusting elegant meals and fancy dresses from her mind. Long hours of grooming, exercising, and training filled the days, giving her little time to dwell on the strange new emotions Travis had aroused. She avoided the reporters who were often hovering around the track and stables, not wishing to be cornered again and bombarded with questions. At night, however, she was less successful in avoiding the dreams that assaulted her awakened senses.

Days passed into weeks, and although Adelia gave all the Thoroughbreds love and attention, she continued to dote on Majesty.

"Don't forget yourself just because you've had your picture in some fancy magazines," she admonished him, failing to keep her voice stern as she completed his grooming.

Paddy strolled into the stables and laid a hand on her shoulder. "Keeping him in line, are you, little

Dee? Don't want him too big for his breeches, do we?"

"That we don't." Turning, she smiled at her uncle, then studied him carefully. "You look tired, Uncle Paddy. Aren't you feeling well?"

"I'm fine, Dee, just fine." He patted her rosy cheek and winked at her. "I think I'll sleep for a week when the Belmont's come and gone."

"You've earned a rest; you've been working hard and long. You're a bit pale. Are you sure—"

"Now, don't fuss," he interrupted with a good-natured scowl. "Nothing worse than a fussing woman. Just be keeping your mind on this lad here." He patted Majesty's side. "Don't you worry about Paddy Cunnane."

She let this pass, vowing silently to keep her eye on him. "Uncle Paddy, is the Belmont important?"

"Every race is important, darlin', and this is one of the top. Now, this fellow here, with that barrel of a chest"—he inclined his head toward Majesty and winked again—"he'll do well there. It's a long race, a mile and a half, and that's what he was bred for. A distance runner, and one of the finest. Not like Fortune, mind you; he's a sprinter and can beat almost anything at a shorter distance. Travis is smart enough to breed horses with both distance and sprinting in mind. That's why he put Fortune in the Preakness at Pimlico, and he was second by half a length. And that's just fine. But this one's for the Belmont." He shook Majesty's head lightly by the muzzle. "And so are you," he added, giving Adelia a pat on the head.

"Me? Am I going as well?"

"That's right. Hasn't Travis told you?"

"Well, no. I haven't seen much of him since we got back from Kentucky."

"He's been busy."

Her answer was absent as she considered the wisdom of attempting to refuse. Recalling the result of her previous attempt, Adelia thought New York might be a fine place to visit.

Belmont Park, on Long Island, was alive with reporters. Adelia managed to stay in the background the majority of the time, and when cornered she escaped as soon as possible. She was unaware of the speculation about her and her relationship with the owner of Royal Meadows' Majesty. The casual attire of jeans and shirt did nothing to conceal the appeal of her beauty, and her reluctance to speak with the press added a mystery that acted as a meaty bone to the hungry pack of reporters. At times she felt hounded and wished she had stood firm and refused to come. Then she would see Travis as he moved toward the stables, hands in pockets, hair ruffled by the breeze. She would admit, though it brought little comfort, that she would have gone mad had she been left behind.

Newspapers and nagging reporters were not in Adelia's thoughts as she joined Travis for the third time in the crowded stands. She noticed, with some discomfort, that Belmont and its occupants were more sophisticated than Churchill Downs. There, size had been offset by an old-world charm, the soft, lazy accent of Louisville. Somehow, Belmont seemed more vast, more intimidating, and beside the sophistication of the elegantly groomed women who occupied the stands and clubhouse, Adelia felt inadequate and naïve.

Silly, she told herself and straightened her shoulders. I can't be like them, and they're certainly taking no notice of me, in any case. Most of these fine ladies can't keep their eyes off Travis. I suppose these are the kind of ladies he sees at his country club, or takes out for a quiet dinner. Depression threatened to settle over her like a black cloud, but she took a deep breath and blew it away.

Adelia had lectured herself that by this time she should be accustomed to the tension and the crush of people, but as post time drew closer she found the familiar anxiety and undeniable excitement capture her. She could find neither words nor ability to speak, and stood gripping the rail with both hands as Majesty strutted to the starting gate. He was impatient, she observed, sidestepping and lifting his front legs in small, nervous prancing steps as Steve struggled to control him, urging him forward into his place in the starting gate.

"I'll have to bring you to the track more often, Dee." Travis gave her shoulder a small squeeze. "In a couple of months, you'll be a veteran."

"I'll never be a veteran, I'm afraid, because each time it seems like the first. I can hardly bear it."

"I'm going to keep bringing you in any case," he informed her, tangling his fingers for a moment in the ends of her hair. "You bring the excitement back. I believe I'd been taking it for granted."

She turned to him, nonplussed by the gentle tone of his voice, and had opened her mouth to speak

when the bell shrilled with the roar of the crowd.
Brilliant silks were now a soft blur as Thoroughbreds
thundered around the track. After the first turn the
field dispersed, transforming from a single mound
of speeding legs to a zigzagging cluster of gleaming bodies. To Adelia, Majesty seemed to weave his
way through them like a fiery comet, passing one
after another until he bore down on the leader. Then,
as if a switch had been flicked, came the power,
the lengthening of stride, the rippling of muscles,
the steady increase of his lead, until Majesty flew
down the home stretch, capturing the coveted
Belmont with power and style.

The crowd went wild, cheering and shouting with
one deafening voice. Adelia's feet left the ground as
Travis lifted her, swinging her in circles as she clung
to his neck. He continued to hold her as Paddy's
arms came around them both, drawing them all
together in joy and excitement. The words shouted
were senseless to her, and she told herself later that
it was the temporary insanity of the moment that
had caused her to meet Travis's lips with hers. Even
on later reflection, she was unclear who had initiated
the kiss, but she knew she had responded. She had
flung her arms around his neck, and the thrill that
had coursed through her had eclipsed even the
rushing flurry of the race. When her feet touched the
ground, and Travis lifted his mouth from hers, her
head was still spinning with light and color, her body
trembling with the backlash of emotion, the tidal
wave of sensation. She could do no more than stare
up at him. For a moment, it was the same as the day
the foal had been born, and the crowded, noisy

stands of Belmont Park faded into a solitary, private world. She was oblivious to the throng and the curious stares, aware only of his arms around her, and the feeling that she was slowly, helplessly, drowning in his eyes.

"We'd best be going down, lad." Paddy made a business of clearing his throat before he laid a hand on Travis's shoulder. Her knees weakened as his eyes left hers to meet her uncle's. She felt the sudden dizziness and disorientation of one who had been awakened from a dream too quickly.

"Yes." Travis grinned, the quick-spreading grin of a boy. "Let's go congratulate the winner. Come on." Spinning Adelia around, he began to lead her away.

"I'm not going down there," she objected, making a futile attempt to hold her ground.

"Yes, you are," he disagreed, not bothering to glance back at her. "I let you have your way before, not this time. You're coming down to help Majesty accept his flowers, white carnations this time, and one's for you."

Her sputtering objections and attempts to disentangle herself went unheeded, and she found herself in the Winner's Circle with the others.

There were microphones and the flash of lights, and she faded into the background as far as possible. She was still shaken by the intensity of need that had flowed through her in Travis's embrace, a strong, wild desire to belong to him completely. It was like being assailed with an unquenchable thirst, and the sensation terrified her. Her morals were deeply rooted, a melding of religious and personal beliefs. She knew, however, that her longing for Travis, her love for him, made her weak, and any resistance would melt as quickly as springtime snow if he pressed his advantage.

She must stay away from him, she determined, avoid situations where they would be alone and she would be vulnerable to his experience and her frailty. As she glanced over at his tall, lean frame, their eyes locked, and she trembled. Her lashes swept down, and she realized helplessly what a rabbit feels when cornered by a strong, sleek fox.

Chapter Six

Back at the hotel, Adelia accompanied Paddy to his room, having no wish to be alone with her thoughts. Travis walked down the carpeted hall with them, pausing at the doorway as they slipped through.

"I've made reservations for us." His teeth flashed in a grin. "Steve's doing his own celebrating with a little lady who's been dogging his footsteps since the Derby."

"Ah, Travis." Paddy sat down heavily on the bed. "You'll have to do without this tired old man. I'm weary to the bone." He gave a smile and a shake of his head. "I've had all the excitement I can stand for today. I'll play lord of the manor and have my dinner in bed like royalty."

"Uncle Paddy." Adelia moved closer, dropping a hand on his brow. "You're not feeling well. I'll stay with you."

"Go on with you." He made a dismissing gesture with his hand. "Fussing like your grandmother used to. It's tired I am, not sick. The next thing I know you'll be pouring some strange remedy down my throat or threatening me with a poultice." He glanced up at Travis with a long-suffering sigh. "She's a worrisome bundle, lad. Take her off my hands and give these old bones a rest."

With a nod of masculine understanding, Travis turned to Adelia. "Be ready in forty-five minutes," he stated simply. "I don't like to be late."

"'Do this, do that,'" she fumed, throwing up her hands. "Never a 'will you' or 'may I.' I'm not in the stables now, Travis Grant, and I don't fancy being ordered about." She tossed back her fiery curls and folded her arms across her chest.

Travis raised a quizzical eyebrow before he moved to the door. "Wear that green thing, Dee. I like it." He closed the door against any possible further outbursts.

Dee was ready at the appointed time, having been cajoled by her uncle to leave him and celebrate Majesty's victory. Telling herself she was only going out with the arrogant brute for Paddy's sake, she zipped herself into the green dress as a knock sounded at her door. Muttering disjointedly about the devil's own spawn, she swung open the door and glared.

"Good evening, Adelia," he greeted her, obviously unconcerned by her warlike stance. "You're looking lovely. Are you ready?"

She glowered at him for another moment, wishing she had something handy to throw at him. Tilting her chin, she stepped into the hall, closing the door with force behind her.

She clung to her stubborn silence as the taxi drove through surging traffic, but Travis remained unperturbed, chatting amiably and pointing out various spots of interest. He was making it very difficult for her to keep her anger on the boil.

Defiance wavered as they entered the restaurant, grander than she could ever have imagined. Wide-eyed, she gazed around her at the sophisticated patrons in their evening dress. She allowed herself to be led unresisting to a quiet corner table, greatly impressed by the elegance of the maître d'. Softly lit and situated for privacy, the table sat high above the throbbing city, the lights blinking and speeding below a direct contrast to their quiet seclusion. She glanced up as their waiter requested her choice of cocktail, then looked across at Travis with a helpless shake of her head. Smiling, he ordered champagne.

"It's a shame we couldn't bring Majesty with us," she commented, then grinned, animosity forgotten. "He did all the work, and we're drinking the champagne."

"I very much doubt he'd appreciate it even if we took him back a bottle. For a royal steed, he has the taste of a peasant. So"—he paused, allowing his finger to rub gently over her hand as it rested on the cloth—"it's up to us to drink to his victory. Did you know, Adelia, the candlelight scatters gold through your eyes?"

Surprised by his sudden observation, she merely stared, greatly relieved when the arrival of the champagne saved her from inventing a response.

"Shall we have a toast, Dee?"

Lifting the slender-stemmed glass, she smiled, more at ease. "To Majesty, the winner of the Belmont Stakes."

His lips curved as he copied her gesture. "To winning."

"Hungry?" he asked after an interlude of quiet conversation. "What's your pleasure?"

"Well, it won't be mutton and potatoes," she murmured absently, sighing at the strange workings of the world that had shifted her into a new life. Her attention came to a full stop as she glanced over the menu, her eyes lifting to his, wide and astonished.

"Is something wrong?"

"It's robbery, sure as faith; there's not another word for it!"

He leaned forward, taking both her hands in his and grinning at her anxious expression. "Are you sure there's no Scots blood in you?" Adelia opened her mouth to retort, highly insulted, but he raised her hands to his lips, causing the words to die before they were born. "Don't get your Irish up, Dee." He smiled over their joined hands. "And overlook the prices. I'm able to deal with them."

She shook her head. "I can't look at it again—it makes my head spin. I'll have what you have."

Chuckling, he ordered the meal and more wine as his hands held hers captive. When they were once more alone, he turned her hands over, examining her palms, ignoring the sharp jerk she made to release herself.

"You're taking better care of them," he murmured, rubbing his thumb over her skin.

"Aye," she retorted, embarrassed and resentful. "They're not quite as bad as a ditchdigger's these days."

He raised his eyes to hers, watching her a moment without speaking. "I offended you that night. I'm sorry." His gentle tone tilted her balance, and she felt the familiar weakness flowing into her.

"It doesn't matter," she stammered and shrugged and tugged at her hands again. He ignored both verbal and physical protests.

"You have fascinating hands. I've made quite a study of them. Small, exquisite, and totally capable—the three rarely go together. Capable Adelia," he murmured before his eyes fastened on hers again with an intensity that caught her off guard. "You had a bad time on that farm, didn't you?"

"I—no. No, we got along."

"Got along?" he repeated, and she felt his eyes searching her face for the words she was not saying.

"We did what needed to be done." She spoke lightly, not sure what it was he wanted from her. "Aunt Lettie was a strong, stubborn woman, and not one to be beaten easily. I often thought it strange how little she was like Da," she continued, her expression drifting into introspection. "And now I see how little she was like Uncle Paddy, for all she was their sister. Perhaps it was the demands of having to take on me and the farm that left her so

little time for the gentler things. Such small things: a
kiss goodnight, a word of affection . . . a child can
starve with a full plate."

She brought herself back with a shake of the head,
surprised by her own words and uneasy under his
glance. She groped for some way to turn the subject.
"I only had the farm to concern me; she had the
farm and me, and I think I was more trouble than
the farm." She smiled, willing him to lighten his
features with one of his own. "She told me a time or
two I had too loose a grip on my temper, but, of
course, I've tightened the hold now."

"Have you?" At last the smile curved his mouth.

"Oh, aye." She gave him a solemn and guileless
nod. "I'm a very mild sort of person."

The smile spread to a grin as their meal was set
before them. As they ate, conversation drifted into
generalities, an easy flow of words, as undemanding
and soothing as the wine that accompanied the food.

"Come," he said suddenly and rose. "Dance with
me."

Before she could voice agreement or protest, she
found herself being led to the dance floor and
enfolded in his all too familiar arms. Her first
stiffness at the contact melted as she relaxed against
him, surrendering herself to his movements and the
quiet music. Surely, she decided, allowing both mind
and body to float, everyone's entitled to a taste of
heaven. Tonight I'm taking mine. Tomorrow will
come, all too soon.

The night was magic, as if a fairy had granted her
a wish, and the very briefness of it heightened her
senses. She tucked all the sights and sensations into a

corner of her mind to be treasured and sighed over when day broke the spell.

It was late when they stepped into the warm night, and though Adelia's eyes were heavy, she wished the evening were just beginning. Clinging to the last enchanted minutes, she made no objection when Travis drew her close to his side in the cab.

"Tired, Dee?" he murmured, his lips brushing the top of her head so lightly she was not sure she hadn't imagined it.

"No," she said on a sigh, thinking how right her head felt cushioned against his shoulder.

He laughed softly, his voice slow and warm, and his fingers stroked through the silk of her hair until her mind drifted into the world of half-dreams.

"Dee?" She heard her name but, loath to rouse herself from the heavenly comfort, she made a small murmur of protest. "We're back," Travis announced, lifting her chin with his finger.

"Back?" Her heavy lids opened, and she stared at the face so close to hers, dreams and reality mixed into confusion.

"At the hotel," he explained, brushing tumbled hair back from her face.

"Oh." She sat up, realizing the dream was over.

He was silent on the elevator ride to their floor, and Adelia used the time to regain her grip on reality. They moved to her door, and Travis removed her key from his pocket to unlock it as she raised her head to thank him. The smile she meant to accompany her thanks faded as she met his eyes. The concentrated, steady look caused her to step backward, only to find herself trapped against the doorframe, while he closed the distance without seeming to move at all. His hand slipped beneath the curtain of her hair, while he caressed her neck in a slow, lazy motion. They gazed silently at each other; then, very slowly, he lowered his head and pressed his mouth to hers in a kiss that was as soft as a summer breeze, unlike the others he had given and ultimately more devastating. She clung to the lapels of his jacket, trying to steady her world, but soon gave up all such efforts and moved her arms to encircle his neck, rising on her toes to meet him demand for demand.

His lips moved to trail along her face, brushing easily along cheeks and closed lids as if savoring the taste. Trembling heat was replaced by a new and poignant languor, a weak giddiness induced by a far more potent potion than champagne. Her hands moved to tangle in his hair as her body melted to his, submitting to whatever he would ask, willing to give whatever he would take.

She felt his hunger when his mouth took hers again, the hardness of his body as he pressed her more urgently against him, and with a moan of pleasure at the new demand, she drew him yet closer. The longing to be possessed, insistent and clamorous, raged through her like fire. She strained against him, her heart throbbing and echoing in her ears as she felt him devour what was offered, then demand more.

Abruptly he released her mouth, his hand moving to brush against her cheek and linger a moment, and she closed her eyes again, inviting his lips to claim hers.

"Goodnight, Dee," he murmured, and, giving her a nudge into the room, he closed the door between them.

Adelia stared at the smooth, empty panel, bringing her hands to burning cheeks. Stunned both by her unprecedented actions and by the sudden rejection, she found it impossible to move. She had offered, and he had refused. Even in her inexperience, she knew her willingness could not have been mistaken for anything other than full surrender. But he had not wanted her, not completely. Her own standards had dissolved in his arms, but he had walked away and left her alone. And how else could it be? she asked herself, shutting eyes tight on threatening moisture. I could never be anything to him but a groom for his horses. Someone who amuses him from time to time. He was only being kind to me, trying to show me a pleasant evening. She trembled once. *I should be content with that and stop searching for what can never be mine.* Glancing down at the soft folds of her dress, Adelia reminded herself she was not Cinderella, and in any case it was long past midnight.

They boarded the plane the next morning in a warm, light drizzle. Again, reporters hounded them. Adelia scurried up the ramp, leaving the men to deal with them. Shaking raindrops from her hair and her cream-colored skirt, she pressed her face to a window and watched Travis disengage himself from the press.

During the flight, she skimmed through a magazine, reluctant to enter into conversation. Travis's

attitude toward her that morning had been casual, friendly, and vaguely preoccupied, and the stir-
ring need in her that lingered from their previous
evening made it a strain for her to mirror his
mood.

When he disappeared into the forward cabin with
Steve, she let out a deep breath and began to pace
the lounge. What am I to do? she asked herself
desperately. How can I control the way he makes me
feel? I'll be making a fool of myself over him; he's
bound to see the way I love him. Then he'll be
feeling sorry for me, and I couldn't stand that. I'll
just have to find a way to keep more distance
between us.

Her gaze wandered over to her uncle, all thoughts
of her problem fleeing her mind as she observed the
unhealthy cast to his normally ruddy skin.

"Uncle Paddy." She moved to him, cupping his
face in her hands and studying him carefully.
"You're not well. What is it?"

"Nothing, Dee." The strain in his voice drew her
brows together. "I'm just tired."

"You're like ice." She knelt down in front of him
so that their faces were level. "You see a doctor the
minute we get home. It won't be long now. I'll fetch
you a cover and a cup of tea."

"Now, Dee, I'm just feeling my age." He stopped
and grimaced in pain.

"What is it?" she demanded, hands already
searching to comfort. "Where are you hurting?"

"Just a twinge." The words came out in jerks
before he began to gasp for air.

"Uncle Paddy! Merciful heaven, Uncle Paddy!"

She clutched at him as he collapsed, falling forward out of the chair and into her arms.

She was not even aware that she shouted for Travis over and over, desperately, helplessly, as she lowered her uncle onto the floor. But suddenly he was there, brushing her hands aside, his head lowering to the stocky chest.

"Tell John to radio ahead for an ambulance," he called to Steve over his shoulder, his hands beginning to push in a steady rhythm on Paddy's chest. "He's had a heart attack."

With a moan, Adelia clutched Paddy's hand to her own heart as if to transfer her strength. "Travis, in the name of heaven—Travis, is he dying? Oh, please, he can't be dying."

"Stop it," he commanded sharply, the words as effective as a slap. "Pull yourself together. I can't deal with this and hysterics as well."

One breath came and went quickly, then she took several more, deep and steady, her hand clutching and unclutching convulsively over Paddy's. Slowly the hysteria was buried under a wall of control, and she began to stroke her uncle's head and speak in soft, reassuring tones, though she knew he probably couldn't hear her.

Seconds dragged and minutes crawled with Travis continually monitoring the unconscious man's pulse, only Adelia's murmurs breaking the silence. She felt the change in the plane's speed and the loss of altitude, heard the whine of the landing gear and felt the jerk of wheels on ground, but her flow of words continued, and she kept her uncle's hand firmly in hers.

She watched through a haze of unreality as paramedics worked on him before transferring him to the waiting ambulance. As she made to join them, Travis took her arm, telling her they would follow in the car. She went without protest, her mind and heart encased in the numbing ice of fear.

She responded only in vague monosyllables to his attempts at consolation, and after a glance at her pale, waxen features, he concentrated on weaving through the traffic toward the hospital.

The long wait began in a small, cheerless lounge scattered with ancient magazines which some read to pass the time and others stared at in desperation. Adelia did neither, but sat, still as a stone, her hands gripped together in her lap, neither moving nor speaking as Travis paced the room like a caged tiger. Her mind was screaming in protest, searching for the power to pray as fear devoured her. Her control was tight, stretching at the seams like an ill-fitting coat as the minutes passed.

When at last a white-coated figure approached, Travis whirled and advanced on him. "You're Padrick Cunnane's family?" the doctor asked, glancing from the tall, powerful man to the small, pale woman.

"Yes." His answer was curt as he too glanced at Adelia. "What's going on? How is he?"

"He suffered a coronary—not a massive attack. He is conscious now, but his condition is aggravated by anxiety over someone named Dee."

Adelia brought her head up. "I'm Dee. Is he going to die?"

The doctor studied the pale, composed features

and took a step closer to her. "We're doing all we can to stabilize his condition, but his own anxiety is a factor in his recovery. His concern is focused on you. I'm going to let you see him. You must do nothing to upset him; persuade him to relax." He turned back to the dark man whose eyes were fixed on the woman. "Are you Travis?" At his nod, the doctor continued. "He wants to see you too. Come with me."

Travis took Adelia's hand and lifted her from the chair, leading her after the retreating white coat.

"Five minutes," the doctor cautioned, and led them into the Cardiac Care Unit.

Her hand tightened in Travis's as she saw her uncle in the hospital bed, wires and tubes joining him to machines that whirled and buzzed. He was pale and drawn and suddenly old, and her mind screamed in revolt as she struggled for control.

"Dee." The voice was weak and unsteady, and she moved close to take his hand in hers.

"Uncle Paddy." Kissing the hand, she held it to her cheek. "Everything's going to be fine. They'll be taking good care of you, and soon you'll be home again."

"I want a priest, Dee."

"All right, don't worry." A cold hand gripped and squeezed her heart, and she felt the trembling start in her knees but forced it away.

"It's you I'm worried for. You can't be left all alone again, not again." His voice was rasping, and she soothed and murmured. "Travis . . . is Travis here?" He continued to fret, and she turned, fear shining from her eyes.

"Right here, Paddy." He moved to stand next to Adelia.

"You've got to take care of her for me, Travis. I'm giving her to you. She'll be all alone again if anything happens to me. Such a wee thing she is and so young. It's been too hard for her. . . . I should have been there for her before. I was going to make it up to her." He made a feeble gesture with his free hand. "I want your word you'll be taking care of her. I can trust you, Travis, with what's mine."

"I'll take care of her; you have my word." His answer was calm and steady, his hand closing over the two that were joined. "You don't have to worry about Dee. I'm going to marry her."

The relaxation in the taut face was visible, his breathing slowing. "You take care of my little Dee, then. I want to see the two of you married. Will you bring a priest here, and let me see it done?"

"I'll arrange it, but you'll have to relax and rest. Let the doctors do their job. Dee and I will be married right here this afternoon. All I need is a judge to sign a waiver of the two-day waiting period."

"Aye, I'll rest till you come back. Till you come back, Dee." She forced her lips into a smile and placed a kiss on his brow before she followed the doctor and Travis from the room. She whirled on him as soon as the door closed behind them.

"Not here," Travis commanded, gripping her arm. "Is there somewhere private we can talk?" he asked the doctor in calm tones. After directing them to an office, the doctor closed the door and discreetly left them alone.

Chapter Seven

Adelia jerked out of Travis's hold as the door shut, fear and despair bubbling into fury. "How could you do that? How could you tell Uncle Paddy you were going to marry me? How could you lie to him that way?"

"I didn't lie, Adelia," Travis returned evenly. "I have every intention of marrying you."

"What are you thinking of, saying such things?" she continued as if he had not spoken. "It's cruel, with him lying there sick and helpless and trusting you. You had no right to make such a promise. You'll break his heart, you—"

"Get hold of yourself," Travis commanded, taking her shoulders and administering a brisk shake. "I told him what he needed to hear, and by God you'll do what he wants if it helps save him."

"I'll not be a party to such a cruel lie."

The grip on her shoulders increased, but she was beyond physical pain. "Doesn't he mean anything to you? Are you so selfish and hardheaded that you can't make a small sacrifice to help him?" She flinched as if he had struck her and turned blindly away, her hands gripping the back of a chair. "We'll stand in that room this afternoon, and we'll be married, and you'll make him believe it's what you want. When we know he's strong enough, you can get a divorce and end it."

She drew her hands over her eyes, pain washing over her in turbulent waves. *Uncle Paddy lying there half dead—Travis telling me we're marrying and divorcing in the same breath. Oh, I need someone to tell me what to do,* she thought frantically.

To be his wife, to belong to him—she'd wanted it so badly that she hadn't even dared to think of it, and now he was telling her that it was going to happen, that it *had* to happen. She was hurt beyond words. It would have been easier to go through life without him than to be his wife for an hour without his love. *Divorce*—he had said it so easily. He was talking of divorce before he had even put the ring on her finger. Taking a deep breath, she tried to force herself to think clearly, but she was too overcome by the bleak realization that he was not talking of a real marriage, a marriage of love, that he didn't want her for herself, but rather for her uncle's sake. There must be another way. There had to be another way. She swallowed painfully to steady her voice, "I'm Catholic. I can't get a divorce," she said dully.

"An annulment, then."

She stared at him in horrified silence, "An annulment?"

"Yes, an annulment. It should not be any problem if the marriage isn't consummated. It will simply be a matter of a little paperwork." He spoke in calm, businesslike tones, and her hands tightened on the chair as she attempted to fight her way through to reason. "For Pete's sake, Dee," he said impatiently, "can't you go through the motions of a ceremony for Paddy's sake? It won't cost you anything. It could make the difference between his living and dying."

He took her shoulders again, spinning her around, checking his anger as he studied the transparent glow to her skin, the fear in her eyes that stared back at him. He could feel the trembling begin under his hands and watched as she shut her eyes and tried to stem it. He muttered an oath, then drew her against him and wrapped his arms around her. "I'm sorry, Dee. Shouting at you is hardly going to make it any easier, is it? Come on, sit down." Leading her to a sofa, he sat beside her, keeping her close inside his arms. "You've been hanging on to control for too long; have a good cry. Then we'll talk."

"No, I don't cry. I never cry. It doesn't help." She held herself rigid in his grasp, but he continued to hold her close. "Please, let me go." She felt her control slipping and struggled against the arms that would not give way. "I have to think. If I just knew what to do . . ." Her breath came in short gasps, the trembling no longer controllable, and her hands clutched at his shirtfront to keep from falling. "Travis, I'm so afraid."

She burst into violent sobs, and his arms tightened around her. Once the tears escaped, she could not stop them. Held in check for more than a dozen lonely years, they now flowed freely down her face pressed into Travis's chest. He kept silent, one hand stroking her hair, and let the storm run its course.

The sobs lost their force, subsiding to soft whimpering, until she lay quiet in his arms, empty and spent. She gave one long, shuddering sigh. "I'll do whatever you think has to be done."

How Travis arranged the paperwork so quickly, she never questioned. She had been too numb to deal with technicalities. The only stand she had made was to refuse to leave the hospital even for a quick rest or a meal. Determinedly, she had planted herself in the waiting room and refused to budge.

She signed her name on the license where she was told, greeted the slender young priest who would make her Travis's wife, and accepted a handful of flowers from a friendly nurse who claimed a woman couldn't be a bride without a bouquet. She smiled at this, a small, frozen smile that hurt her cheeks, knowing she was not really a bride. Legally she would bear the name of the man she loved, but the vows they would exchange would mean nothing to him. The words and motions were only a charade to bring comfort to a sick man.

They stood side by side in the stark room, surrounded by machines, the air heavy with the smell of medicine, and became husband and wife. Adelia repeated the priest's words in a calm, clear voice and looked blankly at the signet ring Travis slipped on her finger before closing her fist over it. It hung loose on her finger and lay like a stone on her heart. In less than ten minutes it was all over, and she accepted his light, brief kiss without demur.

Adelia Cunnane Grant bent over and kissed her uncle's brow. He smiled up at her, his eyes lighting with a suggestion of their usual merriment. She knew in that instant that Travis had been right.

"Little Dee," he murmured, seeking her hand and clinging to it. "You'll be happy now. Travis is a good man."

She forced a smile and patted his cheek. "Aye, Uncle Paddy. You'll rest now, and we'll be able to bring you home soon."

"I'll rest," he agreed, and his eyes raised above her head to meet Travis's. "Treat her with care, lad . . . she's a Thoroughbred."

They drove home in silence. The sun broke through patches of clouds to filter on the road. Adelia watched the play of light and kept her mind a blank. Pulling up in front of the main house, Travis broke the heavy silence.

"I called ahead and informed my housekeeper of the wedding. She'll have prepared your room by now. Your things have been brought over."

She frowned. "I'm not—"

"For the time being," he cut in, his eyes narrowing, "you are my wife, and as such you will live in my house. We'll keep separate bedrooms," he added in a tone that caused her mouth to shut quickly. "We will, however, maintain the outward appearance of a married couple. There is no reason for the present that anyone other than you and I know of this arrangement. Explanations now would only complicate matters."

"I see. You're right, of course."

He sighed at the strain in her voice and went on in gentler tones. "I'll make it as easy on you as possible, Dee. I only ask that you play your part; otherwise you'll be free to do as you please. There'll be no need for you to work,"

"I can't work with the horses?" Adelia broke in, eyes widening in dismay. "But, Travis—"

"Adelia, listen to me." He cupped her face in his hand. "You can do as you like. You don't even know what that means, do you?" His brows drew together at her blank, bewildered face. "If you want to work with the horses, you're free to do so, but not as my employee, as my wife. You can spend your time lounging around the country club or cleaning out stalls—it's up to you."

"All right." Slowly, she unclenched the fists that were tight in her lap. "I'll do my best to make it easy on you as well. I know you were right to do this for Uncle Paddy, and I'm grateful to you."

He stared at her for another moment, then shrugged and slipped from the car.

When they entered the house, a plump, gray-haired woman bustled into the hall to greet them, wiping her hands on a full, white apron.

"Hannah, this is Adelia, my wife."

Warm hazel eyes inspected Adelia and smiled in approval. "Welcome, Mrs. Grant. It's about time a lovely young thing lured my Travis to the altar." Adelia murmured something she hoped was appropriate. "I'm sorry to hear about Paddy; we're all fond of him." The treacherous tears started again, and Adelia closed her eyes against them. "Oh, the poor thing's dead on her feet. Travis, take her up; the room's ready for her."

She started the climb up the staircase, which seemed to take on the proportions of Mount Olympus. Without a word, Travis swept her into his arms and carried her up the remaining steps and down a long, carpeted hallway. Entering a bedroom, he crossed the floor and laid her on a huge four-poster bed.

"I'm sorry." She lifted her hand and dropped it again. There seemed to be nothing further to say.

He sat next to her and brushed the hair from her cheeks.

"Adelia, when will you learn weakness is not always a flaw? Darned Irish stubbornness," he muttered, frowning down at her. "I'd swear nothing else kept you on your feet this long. There hasn't been a whisper of color in your cheeks for the past six hours."

She stared up at him, wanting to pull him down to her and feel the comfort of his warmth. He turned abruptly and moved to a large cherrywood wardrobe.

"I don't know where Hannah put your night clothes." Pulling open the double doors, he exposed the meager contents. "Good heavens, is this all you have?"

She tried to snap at him, but found gathering the strength too great an effort. Moving over to a mirrored triple dresser, he began opening drawers, muttering and swearing, and she lay back and watched him, too weary to be embarrassed that he should handle her clothes with such familiarity.

He pulled out a plain, high-necked cotton gown and, after a brief disparaging scrutiny, brought it to her. "Tomorrow, for heaven's sake, go shopping and buy some clothes."

"Don't you order me about, Travis Grant." She sat up, unable to keep quiet any longer, and snapped at him with a ghost of her usual spirit.

He stared down at her without expression. "While we're married, Adelia, we'll be expected to socialize, and you'll have to dress properly. We'll see to it tomorrow. Now, can you manage to change by yourself, or do you need some help?"

Snatching the gown from his hands, she spoke stiffly. "I can manage very well."

"Good. Change and get some rest. You won't do Paddy any good if you make yourself ill." Without waiting for her reply, he turned and strode from the room, shutting the door behind him.

Too tired to appreciate the beauty of the light, airy room, she slipped off the skirt and blouse which had served as her wedding dress and pulled the cotton nightgown over her head. Folding down the mint-green spread, she crawled between the smooth sheets and fell instantly into the deep, dreamless sleep of exhuastion.

The birds woke her, as was their habit, chattering and chirping outside the window. Opening her eyes, she focused on the unfamiliar surroundings and remembered. She relaxed the fist that had remained tight over her wedding ring throughout the night,

while her eyes made a slow survey of the room. She
had thought her bedroom in the garage house large,
but she estimated this would hold two rooms that
size. The walls were muted green and white striped
paper, trimmed with dark woodwork. The furniture
was cherry, both the large wardrobe and dresser in
which Travis had rummaged the evening before, and
a small writing desk, two night tables and a small
pie-crust table which served a tufted-back chair. On
the small table was a vase bursting with fresh
flowers. Their scent drifted to her as she sat up in
bed, hugging her knees close. She sighed as she
gazed at the tall French windows which led to the
balcony, thinking she had never seen such a lovely
room. *How happy I could be here if only Uncle
Paddy was well, and Travis . . .* She tried to clear her
mind of such negative thoughts. Thrusting back the
covers, she jumped out of bed.

After showering and dressing in her only remaining skirt, she ventured downstairs, hoping she could
locate the kitchen in the strange house which was
now her home.

"Good morning, Dee." Travis appeared from a
room off the downstairs hall which she later learned
was his office. "Feeling better?"

"Aye," she answered, suddenly shy and uncertain
in front of the man who was her husband. "I don't
know when I've slept so long."

"You were exhausted." She kept herself still as he
lifted her chin and examined her face like a parent
seeking to find signs of ill health in a child. "Your
color's back," he said at length and smiled.

"I'm fine." She managed to remain passive as his

hand continued to hold her chin. "I was wondering if I could call the hospital . . . and see if Uncle Paddy—" Her hands fluttered, then clung together in front of her.

"I've already called; his condition has stabilized." His hands moved to rest on her shoulders. "He spent a peaceful night."

A tremor passed through her. She shut her eyes and buried her face against Travis's chest. After a moment, she felt his arms encircle her lightly. "Oh, Travis, I thought he was going to die. I was afraid we would lose him."

He held her away until she tilted her head to look up at him. "He's going to be all right, with a little time and care, and no worries." His features relaxed. "Of course, when he gets home, he'll have to slow down. We'll have to bully him into it."

"Aye." Her smile was like the stars through the clouds. "But there's two of us."

"So there are," he murmured, then tousled her hair. "I imagine you're starving. I couldn't wake you for dinner last night."

"I feel like I haven't eaten in a week." With a sigh, she pushed at the hair he had just ruffled. "If you'll show me the kitchen, I'll start breakfast."

"Hannah's seeing to it," he informed her, taking her arm and leading her into a large dining room. Noticing the expression on her face, he whispered confidentially in her ear as he pulled out a chair, "Don't worry, I've been eating her cooking all my life."

"Oh, I didn't mean—I meant no disrespect. It's

only that I'm not used to having someone fix my meals." Her expression bordered on horror, and he leaned back in his chair and laughed.

"Don't look so stricken, Dee. Hannah will think I'm beating you already."

"Well, I wouldn't want you to think that I meant . . ." She fumbled for something to say which would release her from her awkwardness. "The room you gave me is lovely. I want to thank you."

"I'm glad you like it."

At his careless response, she was grateful for Hannah's entrance with a steaming breakfast platter.

"Good morning, Mrs. Grant. I hope you're feeling better after a good night's rest." She set the platter on the table and Adelia smiled up at her.

"Thank you, I feel fine." She was careful not to start at her new title.

"Hungry though, I'll be bound." Nodding, she studied the pixielike face. "Travis told me you ate next to nothing yesterday, so I'll expect you to do full justice to your breakfast."

"You should be warned, Dee, not to trifle with Hannah," Travis put in from across the table. "She can be ferocious. Personally, she terrifies me."

"Don't you listen to his nonsense, Mrs. Grant." She sent Travis a scowl before giving her attention back to Adelia. "You'll be busy for a while with Paddy in the hospital, but once you're settled, you let me know how you want things done. For now, if it's agreeable, I'll just plan your meals around your visits to the hospital."

"I—whatever you think best."

"We'll have plenty of time to talk about it," the housekeeper concluded. "Now, you get to your breakfast while it's hot." With this she bustled from the room.

Adelia listened to Travis's breakfast conversation, answering only when it was required, while she slowly took in her surroundings. The dining room was large with dark wainscoting and elegantly patterned wallpaper. The furniture was heavy, gleaming oak. Everywhere was the glow of silver and glimmer of crystal.

"Travis," she said suddenly, and his brows rose in acknowledgment as he sipped his coffee. "I don't fit into all this. I haven't the way or the experience to know what's expected of me. I don't want to be an embarrassment to you, and I'm mortally afraid I'll do or say something horrible, and—"

"Adelia." The one word stopped her rambling. She saw from his expression that she had already made a mistake. From the way his face was set, she waited for him to rant at her, but when he spoke, his voice was calm and precise. "You will not embarrass me, you could not embarrass me. Relax and be what you are, that's what's expected of you."

They lapsed into silence. Adelia toyed with the remainder of her eggs. "By the way," Travis began, and she raised her eyes and saw he was smiling, "you've had your picture in the paper."

"My picture?"

"Yes." His smile widened at her frowning expression. "Two pictures, as a matter of fact. There's one of you and Steve with the two of you sitting on the paddock fence, and there's one of you and me taken after the Belmont Stakes.''

Color flooded her cheeks as she realized the contents of the second picture. "I don't know why they kept following me around with their cameras and their pencils."

"I can't imagine," Travis returned, his lips curving again. "It appears that the press has had a splendid time speculating about the romances of my attractive groom. . . ."

Her eyes widened, and the color ebbed and flowed again. "Are you meaning . . . Oh, what a passel of nonsense! Steve and I are friends, and you and I . . ." She faltered, sputtered and fell into excruciating silence.

"Married, Adelia, is what we are, friends or not." With what she thought was a very odd smile, he drained his coffee and rose. "I don't suppose it will sound like such a passel of nonsense to the press when our current relationship is leaked to them. I can keep it out of the papers for a while, but we'll have to deal with it sooner or later. . . . I take it you're done since you've been playing with your fork for the last ten minutes." Securing her arm, he brought her to her feet. "Now, if you'll take that frown off your face, I'll drive you to the hospital."

Any anxiety Adelia still harbored was dispelled by the appearance of her uncle. The color in his cheeks, which had appeared a ghastly gray the day before, was now closer to his normal, ruddy hue. His eyes twinkled as Travis brought her into the room. His voice was weak rather than booming, but steady and unforced. When he complained about being hooked up to blasted, noisy machines, her concern melted into laughter, and, kissing the hand she held in hers, she felt the last vestige of tension dissolve.

After a short visit, Travis drew her into the hall. "You won't be able to stay too long this time. The doctor says he tires easily and needs his rest. That, and seeing you, is the best medicine he can get."

"I won't tire him, Travis," she promised. "He's looking so much better, I can hardly believe my eyes. I'll only stay a little while more. As soon as I see he's tiring, I'll go."

He looked down at her smiling face, his fingers tangling absently with the ends of her hair. "I have to get back now, but Trish will be along soon to take you shopping." His hand dropped, and he stared past her as if suddenly preoccupied. "She'll know best what you need, and if you like she can bring you back here for a while longer this afternoon."

"It's kind of you to be doing all this, Travis." She touched his arm to bring his attention back to her. "I don't know how to repay you for all that you've done already."

"It's nothing." He shrugged off her thanks and, drawing out his wallet, handed her some bills. "I've made arrangements for you to charge whatever you need. Trish will be there to see to the details, but you'll need some cash as well."

"But, Travis, it's so much, I can't . . ."

"Don't argue, just take it." He closed her hands

over the bills in a final, impatient gesture. "Give it to Trish to hold for you, and for heaven's sake, Dee," he added with exasperation, "buy yourself a purse. I'll see you this evening."

He strode down the long corridor, leaving Adelia staring after him.

Chapter Eight

When Trish arrived she greeted Paddy with an affectionate kiss and told him firmly that anyone could see he was faking and enjoying being the center of attention. After a brief visit, she hurried Adelia out into the corridor and hugged her with enthusiasm.

"I'm so happy about you and Travis." Her eyes shone with affection. Adelia began to feel the first weight of guilt. "Now I have the little sister I always wanted." Adelia was treated to yet another hug. "Jerry sends his best." She referred to her husband, her face wreathed in smiles. "The twins went wild when I told them that Dee was now their aunt. They claim that makes them Irish and soon they'll be fey, too."

Adelia responded with smiles and agreeable murmurs, hating herself for the deception and wishing with all her heart that she could confide in the woman whom she felt was a true friend. But she had given Travis her word and she would keep it.

Hooking her arm through Adelia's, Trish began to stroll toward the elevator. "Travis has given me firm instructions to see that you buy a complete wardrobe." She grinned with obvious pleasure as the elevator began its slow descent to the ground floor. "Of course I told him that I would be more than happy to follow orders and spend his money with abandon."

"He said you should hold this for me." Dee handed Trish the wad of bills, which she accepted and placed absently in her tan leather bag. "This is going to be fun."

Adelia smiled faintly.

If Adelia was under the impression that this shopping expedition would follow along the lines of her first, she was soon enlightened to the contrary. Trish ignored department stores for the more exclusive shops. Adelia began to feel as if she were caught in the backlash of a tropical storm. She was whirled through shops while Trish made selections, dismissed or accepted articles with a nod or murmur to the sales clerks. Purchases mounted into an alarming mountain, leaving Adelia dizzy and confused.

Evening dresses that shimmered and flowed, sportswear Adelia considered suitable for royalty, soft, cobwebby lingerie that seemed too fragile to be real; all were tried on, inspected thoroughly by

Trish's critical eye, then approved or rejected. Italian shoes and handbags, French scarves and negligees were included with a nod for foreign craftsmanship.

"Trish, surely Travis didn't mean for me to buy all this," Adelia objected, looking uneasily at the stacks of boxes and bags. "One person couldn't live long enough to wear all those clothes."

"You'd be surprised," Trish murmured absently as she surveyed a long, sweeping evening gown in brilliant green silk. "You'll be doing a lot of traveling, and there are parties and official functions . . ." Her voice trailed off as she held the gown in front of Adelia and narrowed her eyes in consideration. "Travis was very specific. He told me to see to it that you have everything necessary and to ignore the arguments you were sure to give me. That is precisely what I'm doing. Here." She thrust the gown into Adelia's hands. "Go try this on. Green is your color."

"We can't buy anything else," Adelia stated flatly, attempting to hold her ground. "There'll be no room in the car for us when the packages are put in."

"Then, little sister, we'll hire a van." Giving her a shove into the dressing room, Trish gave her attention to a white linen blouse.

Late that afternoon, Adelia stared at the packages that lay piled high on her bed. With a weary sigh, she turned and left the room. Hannah greeted her as she stood in the downstairs hall, unsure whether she should stay in the house or seek out Travis at the stables.

"Mrs. Grant, how's Paddy?"

"He's looking just wonderful. I left him only an hour ago."

"You poor thing, you look all in."

"I've been shopping. I think cleaning out the entire stable would be less of a chore."

Hannah chuckled. "A cup of tea is what you need. Just sit down and I'll bring you one."

"Hannah." She stopped the plump woman before she could bustle away. "Could I . . . would you mind if I came into the kitchen and had one with you?" She made a small, helpless gesture with her hands. "I'm not used to being waited on."

The round face brightened, and a motherly arm slipped around Adelia's waist. "Just you come with me, missy. We'll have a nice cup of tea and a little chat."

It was there Travis found them together an hour later. He stood in the doorway watching in amused amazement as Adelia and Hannah worked on dinner preparations, chattering like lifelong partners.

"Well, well, well, a miracle in this day and age." Two heads turned toward him as he gave his brief, charming grin. "I never thought I'd live to see the day when you'd let anyone work in your kitchen, Hannah." He glanced from his housekeeper to the small woman at her side. "What kind of Irish charm did you use on her, Dee?"

"Just her charming self, you young rascal," Hannah stated with great dignity. "Now, missy"—she removed the vegetable parer from Adelia's hand— "you just run along now and keep that man out from under my feet. He's always been a nuisance in the kitchen."

Travis grinned again, serenely unperturbed. "Come out on the terrace, Dee," he invited and captured her hand. "It's too nice to stay indoors."

He led her out through wide French doors and onto the smooth stone surface of the terrace. The sweet scent of plants and flowers filled the June evening. The sun still cast a warm golden light, scattering shadows on the stone.

"So, Dee," he began, seating her in a striped cushioned chair and dropping down in an identical one across from her, "did you get everything you needed?"

"Everything?" she repeated. She closed her eyes and shuddered. "Never in my life have I ever seen so many clothes, much less put them on. Trying on this, taking off that." Opening her eyes again, she met his wide smile with a look of disdain. "You won't be smiling when you have to build another room to hold them all. Your sister is a stubborn woman, Travis Grant. She just kept tossing things at me and shoving me into dressing rooms. I couldn't make her listen to reason."

"I thought Trish might be helpful."

"Helpful?" She gave a long-suffering sigh. "I felt like I was being blown about by a whirlwind. Packages growing like a great mountain, and Trish smiling and finding something else. She had a fine time," she added, mystified.

"Yes, I imagine she did. I don't see her having much trouble filling out your wardrobe." He smiled at the picture and leaned back in his chair.

"Travis," she began after a small pause, "whatever will I do with all those things?"

"You might try wearing them," he suggested. "It's the usual procedure."

"That's fine for a time. I understand I can't go about in my old clothes with things as they are now. But after, when . . ." She stumbled and searched for the right words. "When things are back as they were before, I—"

"The clothes are yours, Adelia," he interrupted with a quick gesture of his hand. "You'll keep them whatever happens. I certainly have no use for them." Rising, he paced the length of the terrace and stared out over the smooth expanse of lawn.

Adelia sat silently, concerned by his anger and bewildered over how she had caused it. She stood and approached him, laying a tentative hand on his arm. "I'm sorry, Travis. That sounded ungrateful; I didn't mean it to. Everything's happening so fast. I don't want to take advantage of what you're doing for me."

"One can hardly call it taking advantage when it's like pulling teeth to get you to accept anything." His shoulders moved and he turned to face her. "Adelia," he said with a sigh somewhere between impatience and amusement, "you are so artless."

She did not question the ambiguity of his words, so relieved was she that his anger had faded and he was smiling at her again.

"I have something for you." Reaching into his pocket, he drew out a small box. "My signet ring was fine in an emergency, but it looks big enough to fit on your wrist."

"Oh." She found nothing else to say as she opened the box and found a small band studded with winking diamonds and glowing emeralds.

He removed the large, masculine ring from her finger and replaced it with the jeweled wedding band. "I'd say that suits a bit better."

"It fits," she murmured inadequately, overcome with the longing to throw her arms around him and cry out her love.

"I've studied those hands enough to make an educated guess as to your ring size." He spoke lightly and, dropping her hand, moved back to his chair.

Swallowing the obstruction in her throat, she followed him. "Travis." She stood in front of his chair, feeling the strangeness of looking down at him. "Travis, you're doing all the giving, and I have nothing for you. I want to . . . Is there nothing I can do for you? Is there nothing you want from me?"

He met her eyes with a long, unfathomable stare until she thought he would not speak at all. "For now, Dee," he said at length, "the best thing you can do for me is to accept what's given and not question it."

She sighed at his answer. "All right, Travis, if it pleasures you."

He stood and took her hand, a finger running over her wedding band. "Yes, it pleasures me. Come inside and we'll eat, and I'll tell you how Majesty sulked for you today."

The next two weeks passed quickly, Adelia's days full between the hospital and the stables. Paddy was moved into a regular hospital room. No longer attached to machines, he improved daily, complaining vigorously about being stuck in bed and poked with needles. The easy friendliness of the men at the stables and the soothing routine of riding and grooming brought a sense of normalcy back to Adelia's life, and at times she almost forgot she was Mrs. Travis Grant.

Travis was kind and casually affectionate, speaking of Paddy's recovery and on the general topic of horses when they took meals together. He left Adelia free to pursue whatever project she chose, making no demands, his attitude tolerant, generous, and distant. She was aware of a subtle change in their relationship, and she found it did not please her. He never raised his voice or criticized, and he never touched her in any way unless strictly necessary. She wished fervently that he would yell at her or shake her, or do something to lose his cool, composed manner. Their relationship was now far less personal than it had been when they had been employer and employee.

She was returning to the house one afternoon, wondering if Travis had returned from a business appointment, when she stopped and gaped at a large, dirty gray mound of fur exploring a bed of marigolds. After a careful study, she concluded that under the grubby fur was a dog of rather alarming size.

"I wouldn't do that if I were you," she said in a quiet voice that had the dog's head jerking up. "Now, don't be running off. I won't hurt you." The dog hesitated, eyeing her warily, and she kept the distance between them and continued to speak. "It's just that I've seen Travis's gardener—a terrifying man he is. And one that wouldn't take kindly to anyone digging at his flowers." She crouched down, and they studied each other eye to eye. "Are you lost, then, or just roaming? I can see by your eyes you're hungry, I've been hungry myself a time or two. Wait here," she ordered and stood. "I'll fetch you something."

Entering the kitchen, she commandeered a large hunk of roast beef. The whine of the vacuum cleaner was audible from the living room, and, deciding it would be foolish to disturb Hannah and vowing to apologize to her after the deed was done, Adelia slipped back outside.

"It's prime beef, my lad, and from the looks of you, you've not seen its kind before." She placed the offering on the grass and stepped back a few paces.

He came forward slowly at first, eyes shifting from the beef to his benefactor until either his confidence or his hunger grew and he threw himself on the unexpected meal. She watched him polish off what would have fed three hungry men, finding enormous pleasure in his appetite.

"Well, now, you've made a pig of yourself, and that's the truth, and you don't look a bit ashamed." She grinned and watched the long tail thump in agreement. "Pleased with yourself, are you?" Before she could move, she found herself flat on her back, trapped under a hundred pounds of appreciation, her face being drenched by a large wet tongue. "Get off me, you great hairy brute!" Laughing, she pushed to no avail and tried to turn her face from the moisture. "Surely there's not a rib that's not cracked, and it's God's truth you've not had a bath since the day you were born."

After much pleading and wriggling, she managed to release herself, staggered to her feet, and surveyed the damage. Her shirt and jeans were covered with dirt, her arms smeared with it. She pushed at her disordered hair and stared down at the dog that sat at her feet, his tongue hanging out in adoration.

"We'll both be needing a bath now. Well—" She let out a deep breath, tilted her head, and considered. "You wait here, and I'll see what can be done about you. It might be best if you were cleaned up a bit before I introduce you."

On the way back to the house, she paused on the terrace to brush at the dirt that covered her.

"Dee, what happened? Were you thrown? Are you hurt?" Travis rushed to her, his hands claiming her shoulders, then moving to stroke her face. She shook her head, thrown off balance by the frantic tone of his voice.

"No, I'm not hurt. Travis, you mustn't touch me—you'll get your suit filthy." She tried to take a step away, only to be caught closer.

"The devil with the suit!" His voice was edged with anger as he pressed her against him, one hand cradling her head.

The small intimacy after so many days of impersonal distance swamped her with pleasure, and her arms encircled his waist before she could lecture herself on the wisdom of the action. She felt his lips tarry in her hair, and she thought, with a brief flash of joy, that if she could only have this much of him from time to time, she would be content.

Suddenly, one hand gripped her shoulder while the other tilted her face back, and she saw temper flame in his face. "What in heaven's name have you done to yourself?"

"I haven't done anything to myself," she said with a show of dignity, shaking off his hand. "We've company." She gestured to the lawn.

His eyes moved past her, narrowed, then returned. "Adelia, what in the name of heaven is *that?*"

"It's a dog, Travis, though I wasn't sure myself at first. The poor thing was half starving. That's why"—she paused and braced herself for the confession—"that's why I gave him the roast beef."

"You fed him?" Travis asked in low, even tones,

"Surely you wouldn't begrudge the poor thing a bit of food. I—"

"I don't care a whit about the food, Adelia." He shook her briefly. "Don't you have any more sense than to fool with a strange dog? You could have been bitten."

Straightening, she glared at the censure in his voice. "I know what I'm about, and I was careful. He needed food, so I gave it to him—the same as I'd give it to anyone who needed it. And as for that, he hasn't a thought in his head about biting anyone." Glancing over, she watched the dog's tail begin to thump the ground again. "There"—she pointed triumphantly—"you see."

"I see it appears you've made another conquest.

No," he said, and turned her firmly to face him directly. "Just how did you get in this condition?"

"Oh, well." She looked up at Travis, back to the dog, and back to Travis again. "You see, after he'd finished eating, he was overcome with gratitude, and he—well, he forgot himself for a minute and knocked me down and sort of thanked me in his way. He's a bit dirty—as you can see."

"He knocked you down?" Travis repeated, incredulously. At his tone, Adelia hurried on. "He's very affectionate, and he didn't mean any harm. Really, Travis, don't be angry with him. See how pretty he is, sitting there now." She glanced over at the dog and saw he was smart enough to blink soulful eyes in Travis's direction. "I told him to wait, and that's just what he's doing. He only wants a bit of affection."

Travis turned back and gave Adelia a long look. "I'm getting the impression you intend to keep him."

"Well, I don't know about keeping him, exactly." She dropped her eyes from him, stared at a spot of dirt on Travis's jacket, and brushed it away.

"What's his name?"

"Finnegan," she responded immediately, then, seeing she had fallen into the trap, looked up frowning.

"Finnegan?" Travis repeated with a sober nod. "How did you come by that."

"He reminds me of Father Finnegan back in Skibbereen, oversized and clumsy but with much inner dignity."

"I see." He moved over, crouched down, and

inspected Finnegan. To Adelia's relief, the dog remembered his manners.

When Travis returned to her, she moistened her lips and launched into her campaign. "I'll take care of him, Travis; he won't be any trouble. I won't let him come in the house and get in Hannah's way."

"There's no need to use your eyes, Adelia." At her bewildered frown, he laughed and tugged her hair. "Lord help the world if you ever realize what you're doing. You're perfectly free to keep him if that's what you want."

"Oh, I do! Thank you, Travis—"

"There are, however, two conditions," he interrupted before she could finish being grateful. "One, that you teach him not to knock you down; he's every bit as big as you are. And two, that he has a bath." He glanced over at Finnegan and shook his head. "Or several baths."

"I think I'm due for one myself." She brushed again without success at the clinging dirt, then lifted her face with a smile. The smile wavered as she found Travis looking down at her strangely.

"You know, Dee, I'm tempted to stuff you in my pocket where I won't have to worry about you."

"I'm small," she agreed, finding it suddenly difficult to breath, "but I think I'm rather too big for that."

"Your size is intimidating."

She frowned, wondering what he could find intimidating about a bare five feet. His hand wandered through her hair, gently for a moment; then, tousling it with casual friendliness, he added, "I believe it would be easier if you didn't continually look fifteen instead of twenty-three. . . . I guess I had better change my clothes before I give you a hand bathing that mountain."

As her marriage approached its third week, Adelia sat in her uncle's hospital room, smiling at him as he spoke with excitement of his discharge scheduled for the following day.

"Anyone would think they'd been torturing you and starving you to death, Uncle Paddy."

"Oh, no, it's a fine place, with good and kind people," he protested. "But a hospital's for the sick and never have I felt better in my life."

"You are better, and it makes me happier than I can say. But"—she paused and gave him a stern look—"you've still got to rest for a while and do as the doctors tell you. You're coming home to stay with Travis and me for a few days, till you can get by on your own."

"Now, Dee, I can't do that," Paddy objected, patting her hand. "You two should be off on your honeymoon, not worrying about the likes of me."

With a great deal of self-control, she managed not to wince at the word *honeymoon* and went on in calm but firm tones. "You'll be coming back with us, and that's the end of it. I didn't even have to ask—Travis suggested it himself."

Lying back against the pillows, Paddy smiled. "Aye, he would. Travis is a fine man."

"That he is," Adelia agreed with a sigh. She forced a bright smile and continued. "He's fond of you, Uncle Paddy. I knew as soon as I saw the two of you together."

"Aye," he murmured. "Travis and I go back a long way. Just a lad he was when I came to work for his father. Poor motherless child, so solemn and straight he was."

Adelia's mind wandered as she tried to picture Travis as a small boy, wondering if he was tall even then.

"Stuart Grant was a hard man," Paddy went on. "He ran the lad harder than the horses he raised. Trish he left to Hannah, barely showing the girl a passing interest, but the boy he wanted molded in his image. Always giving orders, with never a kind word or a dab of affection.

"I found myself taking the lad in, telling him stories and making games out of the work we did." He grinned, lost in memory. " 'Paddy's Shadow,' the hands called him, 'cause he took to following me about whenever his father wasn't there. He worked hard, and he knew the horses even then. A fine, good lad he was, but the old man couldn't see it. Always finding fault. I wondered sometimes when he grew older why he didn't lay the old man out, goodness knows he was big enough, and the temper was there. But he took the abuse the old man handed him and only looked at him with his eyes so cold." Paddy paused and let out a long breath.

"Travis was away at college when the old man passed on . . . that would be about ten years ago. He stood there looking down at the grave, and I went over and laid my hand on his shoulder. 'I'm sorry about your father, lad,' says I, and he turned and looked down at me. 'He was never my father, Paddy,' says he, just as calm as you please. 'You've been my father since I was ten years old. If you hadn't been there, I'd have left a long time ago and never looked back.'"

The room was suddenly silent. Adelia gripped the hand that lay in hers tighter as Paddy's eyes grew moist with memory. "And now the two of you are together, I couldn't have wished it any better."

"You'll stay with him, Uncle Paddy, always, no matter what? You'll promise me that?"

He turned to her, surprised by the urgency in her tone. "Of course, little Dee. Where else would I be going?"

Chapter Nine

The following evening, after Paddy was comfortably settled into his room in the main house, Travis announced plans for a party.

"It's expected after Majesty's win, but with Paddy's heart attack it's had to be postponed." He swirled a glass of after-dinner brandy, his eyes sweeping over her, resting for a moment on her hair shimmering on the shoulders of her Nile blue dress. "Our marriage has, of course, leaked to the press, and it will seem odd if we don't have some sort of gathering where you can meet some of my friends and business associates."

"Aye," Adelia agreed, unconsciously nibbling on her lip as she turned to gaze out the window. "And so they can get a look at me."

"That too," he answered in solemn tones. "Don't

worry, Dee: as long as you don't trip over your feet and fall on your face you should get by fairly well."

She whirled around to rage at him that she wasn't exactly a clumsy fool, but his good-natured grin stopped her. "Thank you very much, Master Grant." She smiled back at him. "It's a great comfort you are to me."

She gasped out loud at the length of the list Travis gave her for the projected reception. There couldn't be less than a hundred, she estimated, staring at the paper.

"You've nothing to worry about," he assured her. "Hannah will handle the details. You're only expected to make polite conversation."

The attempt at reassurance hurt her pride. "I'll have you know I'm not a complete cabbagehead, Travis Grant. I'm well capable of helping Hannah, and I won't be making a fool of myself in front of your fancy friends."

"You're the one who said she was afraid of making a fool of herself, not me," Travis reminded her reasonably.

"It's not what I said that matters," she concluded with her own brand of logic. "It's what I'm saying." Tossing her head, she turned and stalked into the kitchen.

Despite her proud claims, Adelia found herself terrified on the evening of the party. There had been no time for nervousness in the days before; she had been too busy with plans and preparations. But now, alone in her room, with only the prospect of dressing ahead of her, she began to feel the first flutter of anxiety.

She chose the green silk gown that Trish had insisted she buy and slipped it carefully over her head. Its classic lines accentuated her softly rounded figure; its deeply scooped neckline revealed a teasing hint of her firm breasts. The silk glowed against the creamy health of her skin. She arranged her hair on top of her head, trying for a more sophisticated style, but gave up in disgust and allowed it to fall loose and full to her shoulders, a fiery auburn waterfall.

Voices were audible in the living room as she descended the stairs. She took several deep breaths before joining Travis and Paddy.

Travis broke off what he had been saying as she entered the room. He rose from his chair. She sought his eyes for approval, but found them strangely veiled and unreadable. She wished that she had chosen one of the other gowns that now hung in the large cherry wardrobe.

"Ah, now, isn't that a beautiful sight, lad?" Paddy said, surveying Adelia with uninhibited pride. "Why, there won't be another woman here tonight will hold a candle to my little Dee. It's a lucky man you are, Travis."

"Uncle Paddy." She smiled and moved to kiss his cheek. "What wonderful blarney. But don't stop—I need it. I have to be honest and say I'm scared witless."

"There's no need for that, Dee." Taking her hand, Travis turned her toward him. "You'll have them eating out of your hand. You look incredible." He smiled at her, his free hand brushing through her hair briefly before he turned away to replenish his drink.

Love me, Travis, her mind shouted suddenly. *I'd give the world and more if you'd only love me half as much as I love you.*

As he turned back, his eyes captured hers. He paused, unreadable emotion flickering over his face. "Dee?" he began, his voice questioning, but before she could speak the doorbell pealed and their guests began to arrive.

It was infinitely easier than Adelia had imagined. After the first wave of guests, she felt her tension dissolve and met the few speculative glances with characteristic boldness. The house was soon filled with people and chatter and laughter and the chink of glasses. It was apparent that Travis was well liked and respected by his associates, and his choice of bride met with acceptance and approval, if not immediately, then shortly after exposure to Adelia's natural, honest charm.

One sleekly coiffured woman who had cornered Adelia halted Travis as he passed. "Travis, your wife is refreshing and charming and more than likely too good for you." She smiled with the privilege of old friendship. "I believe it would be a treat just to listen to her read the telephone directory. Such a marvelous accent."

"Careful, Carla," Travis admonished, slipping an arm around Adelia's shoulder in the casual way she had missed in the past few weeks. "Dee claims we're the ones with the accent—and for all her sweet looks, her temper is not to be trifled with."

"Travis, darling!" The trio turned, and Adelia caught a glimpse of swirling white as the owner of the voice embraced her husband. "I just got back in town, darling, and heard about your little party. I hope you don't mind."

"Of course not, Margot. It's always a pleasure to see you." He turned, and Adelia noted that he didn't dislodge the red-tipped hand from his arm. "Margot Winters—my wife, Adelia."

Margot turned, and Adelia nearly gasped aloud. She was staring right at the most beautiful woman she had ever seen. Tall and slender, she was elegantly draped in a cool white sheath. Ash-gold hair curled softly around an oval face. Her skin was the color of rich cream. Long-lashed gray eyes, as clear and cool as a mountain lake, looked over and beyond Adelia.

"Why, Travis, she's adorable." The gray eyes focused now on Adelia, making her feel small and inadequate. "But she's little more than a child, barely out of the schoolroom." The sweet tone was patently patronizing.

"I'm allowed up with the grown-ups now and again," Adelia said evenly, her chin tilting to meet Margot's gaze. "I hung up my book strap some time back."

"My," Margot observed over Carla's chuckle. "You're Irish, aren't you?"

"Aye." The quicksilver temper began its swift rise. "As Paddy's pig. Tell me, Mistress Winters, what are you?"

"Dee." Trish spoke from behind, laying a hand on

Adelia's arm. "Will you come out here for a minute? I need you to help me."

Adelia was pulled out on the terrace, and after she had shut the doors, Trish dissolved into a fit of laughter. "Oh, Dee," she managed between giggles. "How I would have loved to have left you there and watched you lay into her! I just didn't think it was quite the right time. Oh . . ." She wiped at her eyes. "Did you see Carla? I thought she was going to explode! She kept choking on her drink and trying to keep a straight face. I wouldn't have missed that for the world! How Travis could ever have been involved with that woman is beyond me! She's a cold-blooded snob."

"Travis and Margot Winters?" Adelia asked, attempting to keep her voice casual.

"Oh, yes, I thought you knew." Trish gave a deep sigh, wiped her eyes again, and grimaced. "I don't really think he was ever serious about her—I give him more credit than that. She would have given one of her Tiffany baubles to have him look at her the way he looks at you." Trish smiled, and Adelia made a valiant effort to respond. "They had this big blowup a few months ago. It seems she resented all the time he spent with the horses." She gave a snort of disgust and straightened her skirts. "She wanted him to sit back and let others do all the work while he spent his time entertaining her. She gave him some kind of ultimatum and took off for Europe in a cloud of expensive French perfume." Trish laughed in pure delight. "Her little ploy failed miserably, and now her nose is out of joint. Instead of pining for her, Travis is happily married to you." She linked her arm with her sister-in-law's.

"Aye," Adelia murmured. "Now he's married to me. . . ." Her tone was melancholy, and Trish glanced at her sharply, but Dee refused to meet her eyes.

Paddy moved back to his own house a few days later, and Adelia missed his presence keenly. He found Finnegan a congenial companion, and the dog divided his time between them. He would accompany Paddy as he grumbled inside for his afternoon rest, and Adelia was never quite sure whether Finnegan's motives were duty or laziness.

Travis made no mention of Margot Winters or Adelia's comments to her, and she found their relationship drifting away again until she felt more like his ward than his wife. When they attended social functions, he treated her with the warm attentiveness expected of a newly married husband; but once they were alone again in their own home, he was distant, showing her only the casual affection he might give to a favored cousin.

The depression and frustration this caused in her Adelia hid with apparent success, responding as she believed he desired and maintaining the same casualness he directed toward her. Rarely did her temper flare, and she was aware his was under strict control. At times she imagined they were only polite puppets pulled on invisible strings. Desperately she wondered how long they could go on.

One afternoon, as July brought summer's throbbing heat to the air, Adelia answered the summons of the bell and found herself confronted with the elegantly clad form of Margot Winters. Her finely penciled brows lifted at Adelia's attire of jeans and shirt. She glided over the threshold without invitation.

"Good afternoon to you, Mistress Winters." Adelia greeted her, determined to act the part of hostess. "Please come in and sit down. Travis is down at the stables, but I'll be glad to send for him."

"That's not necessary, Adelia." Margot strolled into the living room and seated herself in a wing-backed chair as if she belonged there. "I came to have a little chat with you. Hannah"—she glanced over at the housekeeper, who had entered behind Adelia—"I'll have some tea."

Hannah looked pointedly at Adelia, who merely nodded and moved to join her uninvited guest.

"I shall come straight to the point," Margot began, sitting back and linking her fingers together in an imperious gesture. "I'm sure you're aware that Travis and I were about to be married before we had a slight disagreement a few months ago."

"Is that the truth of it?" Adelia asked with apparently idle interest.

"Yes, it was common knowledge," Margot stated with a regal wave of her hand. "I thought to teach Travis a lesson by going to Europe and giving him time to think things through. He's a very stubborn man." She gave Adelia a small knowing smile. "When I saw the picture of him in the paper kissing this little ragamuffin, I thought nothing of it. The press will blow these things out of proportion. But when I heard he'd actually married some little stablehand"—she shivered delicately—"I knew it was time to come back and set things straight."

"And may the stablehand ask how you mean to do that?"

"When this little interlude is finished, Travis and I can proceed as planned."

"And by interlude I suppose you're meaning my marriage?" Adelia inquired, her voice lowering to an ominous level.

"Well, of course." Slender shoulders moved at the inevitable. "Just look at you. It's obvious Travis only married you to bring me back. You can't possibly hope to hold him for very long. You haven't the breeding or style that's necessary to move in society."

Straightening her spine, Adelia hid her pain with dignity. "I'm telling you this as a fact, Mistress Winters: you had nothing to do with the reason that Travis and I were married. It's true I haven't your elegance or manner of speaking, but there's one thing I have you're lacking. I've Travis's ring on my finger, and you'll be having a good long wait before you can add his name to yours."

Hannah entered bearing a tea tray, and Adelia rose and turned to her. "Mistress Winters won't be staying for tea after all, Hannah. She was just leaving."

"Play the lady of the house while you can," Margot advised, rising and gliding past Adelia's stiff form. "You'll be back in the stables sooner than you think." When the door closed with a sharp bang, Adelia let out a deep breath.

"She's got her nerve coming here and talking that way," an irate Hannah sputtered.

"We'll be paying her no mind." She patted the housekeeper's arm. "And we'll keep this visit between the two of us, Hannah."

"If that's the way you want it, missy," Hannah agreed with obvious reluctance.

"Aye," she replied, staring off into space. "That's the way I want it."

Adelia's nerves remained on edge for several days and showed all too plainly in increased temper. The atmosphere in the house went from a near-stagnant calm to volatile motion. Travis greeted her change in attitude with absent tolerance that changed to strained patience.

She paced the living room after dinner one evening while he sat on the sofa and brooded over his brandy.

"I'm going to take Finnegan and go for a walk," she announced suddenly, unable to bear the silence between them any longer.

"Do as you like," he answered with a shrug.

" 'Do as you like.' " She whirled and snapped at him, nerves as tight as an overwound watch. "It's sick to death I am of hearing you say that. I will not do as I like. I don't want to do as I like."

"Do you hear what you just said?" he demanded, setting down his brandy and staring at her. "That is the most ridiculous statement I have ever heard."

"It's not ridiculous. It's perfectly clear if you had the sense to understand it."

"What's gotten into you? You make more sense when you mutter in Gaelic."

"Nothing," she returned shortly. "There's not a thing wrong with me."

"Then stop behaving like a shrew. I'm tired of putting up with your foul temper."

"A shrew, am I?" Her color rose.

"Precisely," he agreed with infuriating calm.

"Well, if you're tired of listening to me, I'll keep well out of your way." Storming from the room, she flew past an astonished Hannah, out the back door, and into the warm summer night.

She awoke the next morning ashamed, disgusted, and contrite. She had spent an uneasy night struggling with the aftermath of temper and the realization that not only had she been unreasonable, she had made a fool of herself as well. One was as difficult to take as the other.

Travis has done nothing to deserve the way I've been treating him, she decided, pulling on her working uniform of jeans and shirt and hurrying downstairs. She determined to apologize and make a study of being as sweet and mild a wife as any man could want.

Hannah informed her that Travis had breakfasted early and gone out, so Adelia sat down in solitary misery, unable to ease her conscience.

She worked hard in the stables that morning, doing self-imposed penance for her faults. And as morning melted into early afternoon, the manual labor began to erase the depression she carried with her.

"Dee." Travis spoke from outside the tackroom

where she was busily hanging bridles. "Come out here. I want to show you something."

"Travis." She ran after him as he strode away. "Travis." Catching up to him, she tugged on his arm in an attempt to make him slow his pace. "I'm sorry, Travis. I'm sorry for the way I've been behaving, and for raging at you last night when I had no cause to. I know I've been mean and spiteful and no fun to have around, but if you'll forgive me, I'll . . . What are you smiling like that for?"

The smile spread to a grin. "You apologize just as emphatically as you rage. It's fascinating. Now, forget it, half-pint." He ruffled her hair and slipped an arm around her shoulders. "Everyone has their black moods. Look," he said simply and pointed.

She gave a cry of pleasure at the glossy chestnut mare prancing around inside the paddock fence. Moving over, she stood on the first rung of fence and scanned the strong, clean lines. "Oh, Travis, she's beautiful—the most beautiful horse I've ever seen!"

"You say that about all of them."

She smiled at him, then back at the horse with a deep sigh of pleasure. "Aye, and it's always true. Who will you breed her with?"

"That's not up to me. She's yours."

Adelia turned wide, unbelieving eyes to his. "Mine?"

"I had thought to give her to you next month for your birthday, but"—he shrugged and brushed a lock of hair from her face—"I thought your spirits needed a lift, so she's yours a bit early."

She shook her head, the still unfamiliar tears filling her eyes. "But after the way I've been acting, you should have been beating me instead of buying me a present."

"The thought entered my mind last night, but this seemed a better solution."

"Oh, Travis!" She flung herself into his arms without restraint. "No one's ever given me such a grand present, and I don't deserve it." She drew her face from his cheek and pressed her lips to his. His arms tightened around her, the kiss changing from one of gratitude to one of smoldering passion, and she offered herself, lips parting and bones melting. "Travis," she murmured as his face lifted, his cheek brushing hers.

He set her away from him abruptly. "You'd better get acquainted with your mare, Dee. I'll see you at dinner."

She watched him stride away, biting her lip to prevent herself from calling him back. Finnegan bounded over, and she swallowed the tears of rejection, burying her face in his fur. "I don't have any appeal for him," she told her sympathetic companion. "And I don't know how to go about making him see me as a woman—much less a wife."

Chapter Ten

Adelia woke to a blinding flash of lightning and a burst of thunder. The room glowed with brief intensity as the sky was broken with spiderwebs of light, and the wind moaned like a man mourning.

Tossing back the covers, she rose from the bed and threw open the French doors leading to her balcony to let the storm enter the room. The hands of the wind pulled at her hair and whipped the soft material of her thin nightgown, molding it against her. Rain fell in torrents like angry tears from the heavens, and she raised her arms wide, laughing in sheer delight at the raging elements.

"Dee?" She turned her head and saw Travis silhouetted in the doorway. "I thought you might be frightened. The electricity's out, and the storm's loud enough to wake the dead."

"Aye," she agreed triumphantly. "It's wonderful!"

"So much for finding you shaking with fear under the covers," he returned with a dry smile and stepped back.

"Oh, Travis, come look!" she cried as another bolt of lightning illuminated the murky sky and was followed by a deafening roar of thunder.

He watched her slimness outlined against the blackness, the fullness of her hair flying riotously around her bare shoulders. He opened his mouth to speak, but Adelia cried out again.

"Oh, come, just look at it!" Taking a deep breath, he moved to join her. "It's so wild, so strong and powerful and free!" She lifted her face to feel the full force of the wind on her cheeks. "It's angry as the devil and doesn't give a hoot what anyone thinks. Listen to the wind, screaming like a banshee! Oooh, but I love a storm that blows free!"

She turned and found his eyes on her. Lightning flooded the room, and she saw the naked desire darkening his unblinking blue stare. Her smile faded. Her heart pounded in her ears, drowning out the turbulence of the storm as he pulled her against him and crushed her lips in a violent, hungry kiss.

Her arms clutched around his waist as they fused together, and she felt the need in him she had not known existed and knew a moment's delirious pleasure that it was for her. Fire ignited fire. Her response was abandoned and uninhibited. His mouth ravished hers, hard and bruising, and she opened under the pressure like a flower to the sun.

His hand slid to her shoulders, and the soft material of her nightgown sighed to the floor. Her hands fumbled with the belt of his robe until no barrier of silk came between them. With a swift, desperate gesture, he lifted her and carried her to the bed.

The passionate violence of the storm paled against the turbulence of their lovemaking. His lips moved over hers slowly, his hands roaming with gentle experience over her trembling body, releasing her desire while he kept his own in check. When he made her his she surrendered, drawing her pleasure from the gift she gave.

Later, she slept in the warm circle of his arms, the deep, peaceful sleep of one who has been lost and searching and finally found home. . . .

Sunlight streamed warm and loving on Adelia's face, and she opened her eyes. Travis's face lay close to hers, and she studied it thoroughly and sighed, her love nearly bursting her heart. His breathing was slow and even, the deep blue of his eyes hidden by lowered lids and lashes which seemed incredibly long and thick against the strongly masculine face. Her hand lifted and stroked the dark curls away from his forehead, and she snuggled closer, murmuring his name.

His eyes opened at her movements and smiled into hers. "Hello," he said simply as his arm tightened around her waist. "Do you always look this beautiful first thing in the morning?"

"I don't know," she answered. "It's the first time I've ever woken with a man on my pillow." She rolled on top of him and peered down at his face critically. "You're not a hard sight on the eyes either." Grinning, she rubbed a hand over his chin. "Though it's a fact you're needing a shave."

He tugged the hair that fell streaming from her head to his shoulders and brought her face down, claiming her lips. After a moment she lay her head in the curve of his shoulder, sighing with absolute contentment as he caressed her back with slow, idle movements. "Travis," she said curiously, "that clock says it's after ten."

He twisted to see for himself and groaned. "That's what it says."

"But it can't be," Adelia objected, raising herself up in indignation. "Why, never in my life have I slept as late as that!"

"Well, you did this time." He grinned. "Even you can't argue the day back."

"I'll pretend I didn't see it," she decided and snuggled against his warmth.

"As much as I'd like to do the same, I have an appointment, and I'm already going to be late." He kissed her again, rolling her over, and she clung to him, moving her hands over the rippling muscles of his back. "I've got to go." His lips tarried a moment at the curve of her neck before he disentangled himself. He rose and slipped on his robe, turning back to gaze at her slim form, scantily covered by rumpled sheets. "If you stay there for a couple of hours, I'll be back."

"You could stay now and be a bit later for your appointment," she suggested with a smile as she sat up, clutching the sheet to her breast.

"Don't tempt me." Moving over, he kissed her brow. "I'll be back as soon as I can."

When the door closed behind him, she lay back with a blissful sigh and stretched. *I'm truly his wife now*, she thought, closing her eyes as memories of the previous night ran through her mind. *I'm a married woman, and Travis is my husband. But he never said he loved me.* She sighed and shook her head. *He said he needed me, and that's enough for now. I'll make him love me in time. I'll make our marriage work, and he'll not be thinking of ending it. I'll make him so happy he'll think he's found heaven.*

She jumped from the bed, full of confidence, and danced into the adjoining bathroom to shower.

Later, she paused halfway down the stairs, her face lighting with pleasure as she heard Travis's voice coming from the living room. Before she could begin the rapid descent she had intended, another voice floated to her, and she stopped, the smile fading as she recognized Margot Winters's voice raised in exasperation.

"Travis, you know very well I never meant those things I said before I left. I only went away so that you'd miss me and come after me."

"Did you expect me to drop everything and run off to Europe chasing you, Margot?" Adelia heard the slight amusement in his tone and bit her lip.

"Oh, darling, I know it was foolish." The voice became low and seductive. "I never meant to hurt you. I'm so terribly sorry. I know you married that little groom to make me jealous."

"Is that so?" The answer was calm, and Adelia's

hand tightened on the banister at his cool, dispassionate discussion of her.

"Of course, darling, and it worked beautifully. Now all you have to do is arrange for a quick divorce and give her a nice little settlement, and we'll get things back to normal."

"That may be difficult, Margot. Adelia's Catholic; she'd never divorce me." Her stomach lurched at the easy remark, and she wrapped her arms around herself to ward off the sharp, piercing stab of pain.

"Well, then, darling, you'll just have to divorce her."

"On what grounds?" Travis's voice sounded reasonable.

"For heaven's sake, Travis." The feminine voice rose in annoyance. "You can arrange something. Give her some money. She'll do what you want."

Adelia could stand no more. Covering her ears with her hands, ran up the carpeted stairs and into her room.

Oh, 'tis a fool you are, Adelia Cunnane, she berated herself, leaning against her door. *He doesn't love you and he never will. Your marriage was just make-believe all along.* She dashed away the tears and straightened her shoulders. Now's the time to end it, she decided firmly. Uncle Paddy's strong enough, and I can't go on this way any longer.

She packed only her old clothes and those bought with her own earnings in the well-battered case she had carried from Ireland, then sat at the writing desk and penned notes to her uncle and husband.

Please understand, Uncle Paddy, she pleaded, placing the two envelopes on the smooth surface of the desk. *I can't be going on with this anymore. I can't stay here so close to Travis, not now, not after all that's happened.*

She slipped downstairs and, taking a deep breath, walked outside to await her taxi.

The airport was as busy as it had been on her arrival, throngs of people rushing around her and shaking her confidence. For a moment she felt achingly lost and alone. Sighting the ticket counter, she drew herself up and headed toward it. A hand gripped her arm and spun her around. She dropped her case to the tiled floor with a thud.

"What do you think you're doing?" she began indignantly, stopping openmouthed as she looked up into Travis's furious face.

"That's precisely what I wanted to ask you," he tossed back, his eyes boring into hers with a hard blue light. "Where do you think you're going?"

"To Ireland, back to Skibbereen."

"Are you stupid enough to think I'd let you get on that plane without a word?" he demanded, his grip on her arm increasing.

She winced at his bruising fingers but answered evenly, "I left you a note."

"I saw your note," he hissed between his teeth. "It's a good thing I got back early, or I'd be chasing you across the Atlantic."

"There's no need for you to be chasing me anywhere," Adelia insisted, pulling at her arm as the circulation began to slow down. "You're breaking my arm, Travis Grant. Take your hand off me."

"You're lucky it's not your neck," he muttered,

and, lifting her case with his free hand, he began to pull her after him.

"I'm not going with you—I'm going back to Ireland."

"You are coming with me," he corrected. "And you can walk on your own two feet, or I'll cart you out like a sack of Irish potatoes."

"A sack of Irish potatoes, is it?" she spat at him, but as he towered over her, formidable and powerful, she tossed her head and went on calmly. "Aye, I'll walk, Master Grant. There'll be other planes."

Muttering an oath, he strode purposefully out to his waiting car, towing her with him. He opened the door and gave her a none too gentle shove inside. "You've got a lot of explaining to do, Adelia," he said as he started the engine. She opened her mouth to retort, but he cut her off with a deadly look. "Save it until we get home. I have no desire to commit murder publicly."

She remained silent on the drive home, stubbornly staring out the side window. Pulling up in front of the large stone house, Travis got out of the car, slamming his door with such force Adelia was amazed that the glass remained intact. He pulled Adelia out and dragged her inside.

"We're not to be disturbed," he announced to a gaping Hannah as he hauled Adelia up the staircase. Pushing her into her room, he slammed the door and locked it. "Now, let's hear it."

"I've an earful for you, Travis Grant," she raged. "You great thundering blackguard, I'm sick to death of your shoving me and pushing me and tearing my arms from the sockets. I warn you, you black-hearted son of the devil, you'll not be battering me about any longer unless you've a mind to have a few bruises of your own!"

"If you've finished," he returned evenly, "I'd like to see you use that double-edged tongue of yours for an explanation."

"I've no need to explain a blessed thing to the likes of you." Her eyes glittered bright green in her furious face. "I told you plain in the note: I want nothing from you. I've my pride if nothing else."

"Yes, you and your Irish pride," Travis growled, stepping forward and taking her by the shoulders. "I'd like to strangle you with your pride. What was all that about divorce and annulments?"

"I thought my wording clear enough." She jerked away and backed up. "I said that, as an annulment was no longer possible, I was leaving and you'd be free to divorce me. I wanted none of your money and would pay you back for what I took with me."

"And you expect me to accept that?" he shouted at her, and she backed up another step. "Just calmly read your little note and go from marriage to divorce in one easy step?"

"Don't you shout at me," she snapped back. "It was agreed when we started that this marriage was only for Uncle Paddy, and we'd have an annulment when he was better. Now that can't be, so you'll have to divorce me. I'm not able to do it myself."

"You can talk of annulments and divorce after last night?" he threw back bitterly. "I thought it meant something to you."

"I can speak of it? I can speak of it?" she roared, out of control. "You dare say that to me? The devil take you, Travis Grant, for your hypocrisy! You'd no more than left the bed when you spoke of divorcing me with your fine lady. Give me money to buy me off, will you? You low, sneaking buzzard! I would rather die than touch one penny of your money, you low-lying snake!"

"Dee, is that why you left?" Travic demanded, shaking her as she resorted to Gaelic curses.

"Aye." Her small fists beat uselessly at his chest. "Take your hands off me, you cursed brute. I'll not wait around to be bought off like some cheap fancy lady."

He picked her up bodily, tucking her like a football under his arm, and ignoring the flailing fists, laid her gently on the bed.

"So it's back to bed again, is it? I'll not lie in this bed with the likes of you again. A curse on you, Travis Grant!"

"Be quiet, you little fool." Travis captured her mouth, shutting off the stream of Gaelic, and held it until her furious struggles lost their force. "Did you think I'd let you go after all I've been through to get you?" He cut off her reply with another breathtaking kiss. "Now, you little spitfire, keep your mouth shut and listen. Margot came here this morning without invitation. She brought up the subject of divorce, not I. In the first place—Keep still," he warned as she squirmed beside him, "or I'll have to get tough." He demonstrated by closing his mouth over hers until, for a moment, her struggles lost their force.

"In the first place," he began again, "I had never considered marrying her; any plans in that direction were her own. We had a fairly compatible relationship for a while—Adelia, *hold still*. You're going to hurt yourself." He shifted his weight, took both of her wrists in his hand, and held them over her head. "She got it into her head that I should marry her and give up my work here, with some crazy notion about traveling the world and living in high style. I told her she was out of her mind, and she took off for Europe, telling me it was her or the horses." He grinned down at Adelia's flushed face. "The horses won, hands down. She got it stuck in that small brain of hers that I married you to spite her, and when she came here this morning going on about divorce and settlements, I let her ramble, curious to see how big a fool she'd make of herself."

He took Adelia's chin in his free hand and held her head still. "Now, if you had listened to the entire conversation, you would have heard me tell her that I had no intention of divorcing a wife I loved, now, or any time within the next thousand years."

"You said that?" All struggles stopped.

"Or words to that effect. The meaning was clear."

"I—well, you might have told your wife you loved her. It would have saved a great deal of trouble."

"How could I tell her I loved her five minutes after she raged at me, standing there looking like an outraged urchin?" He brushed her curls aside to kiss the creamy skin of her throat. "My first thought was to gentle you so you could stand the sight of me and go from there. Did you really think I took you to Kentucky and New York just for Majesty?" His lips explored her smooth skin. "I didn't dare let you out of my sight; someone might have come along and snatched you away. I decided to wear you down slowly." His mouth moved over her face with slow, lingering kisses. "I thought I was making some headway, but Paddy's heart attack changed everything. I felt the best way to help him was to assure him of your welfare, so I railroaded you into marriage with the promise of an annulment. Of course"—his free hand began fresh explorations—"I never intended to give you one."

"Let go of my hands," she demanded, and he raised his head and shook it.

"Not if I have to keep you here for the next twenty years."

"You thick-brained idiot, couldn't you see how I was dying for loving you? Let go of my hands, blast your eyes, and kiss me."

She pulled his head to hers with her freed hands, and buried her face in the strong column of his neck.

"It appears," he murmured in her scented hair, "we've wasted a great deal of time."

"You seemed so far away. All those weeks you never even touched me. You never even said you loved me last night."

"I didn't dare touch you. I wanted you so much it was driving me mad. If I had told you I loved you last night—and how I wanted to!—you might have thought I said it just to keep you in bed."

"I won't think that now, Travis. Let me hear you

say it. I've been needing to hear you say it for such a long time."

He obliged her, telling her over and over until his lips sought hers and told her silently.

"Travis," she finally whispered against his ear. "I'm wondering if you could arrange another thunderstorm?"

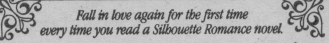

*Fall in love again for the first time
every time you read a Silhouette Romance novel.*

If you enjoyed this book, and you're ready to be carried away by more tender romance...get 4 romance novels FREE when you become a Silhouette Romance home subscriber.

Act now and we'll send you four touching Silhouette Romance novels. They're our gift to introduce you to our convenient home subscription service. Every month, we'll send you six new Silhouette Romance books. Look them over for 15 days. If you keep them, pay just $11.70 for all six. Or return them at no charge.

We'll mail your books to you two full months *before they are available anywhere else.* Plus, with every shipment, you'll receive the Silhouette Books Newsletter absolutely free. *And Silhouette Romance is delivered free.*

Mail the coupon today to get your four free books—and more romance than you ever bargained for.

Silhouette Romance is a service mark and a registered trademark of Simon & Schuster, Inc.

— — — — **MAIL COUPON TODAY** — — — —

Silhouette Romance®
120 Brighton Road, P.O. Box 5020, Clifton, N.J. 07015

☐ Yes, please send me FREE and without obligation, 4 exciting Silhouette Romance novels. Unless you hear from me after I receive my 4 FREE books, please send me 6 new books to preview each month. I understand that you will bill me just $1.95 each for a total of $11.70—with no additional shipping, handling or other charges. **There is no minimum number of books that I must buy, and I can cancel anytime I wish.** The first 4 books are mine to keep, even if I never take a single additional book.

☐ Mrs. ☐ Miss ☐ Ms. ☐ Mr.   BRR9L9

Name _____ (please print)

Address _____ Apt. No. _____

City _____ State _____ Zip _____
(   )
Area Code   Telephone Number

Signature (If under 18, parent or guardian must sign.)

This offer, limited to one per household, expires November 30, 1984. Prices and terms subject to change. Your enrollment is subject to acceptance by Simon & Schuster Enterprises.

Let Silhouette Inspirations show you a world of Christian love and romance... for 15 days, free.

If you want to read wholesome love stories...with characters whose spiritual values are as meaningful as yours...then you'll want to read Silhouette Inspirations™ novels. You'll experience all of love's conflicts and pleasures—and the joy of happy endings—with people who share your beliefs and goals.

These books are written by Christian authors...Arlene James, Patti Beckman, Debbie Macomber, and more...for Christian readers. Each 192-page volume gives you tender romance with a message of hope and faith...and of course, a happy ending.

We think you'll be so delighted with Silhouette Inspirations, you won't want to miss a single one! We'd like to send you 2 books each month, as soon as they are published, through our Home Subscription Service. Look them over for 15 days, free. If you enjoy them as much as we think you will, pay the enclosed invoice. If not, simply return them and owe nothing.

A world of Christian love and spirituality is waiting for you...in the pages of Silhouette Inspirations novels. Return the coupon today!

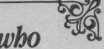

For the woman who expects a little more out of love, get Silhouette Special Edition.

Take 4 books free – no strings attached.

If you yearn to experience more passion and pleasure in your romance reading ... to share even the most private moments of romance and sensual love between spirited heroines and their ardent lovers, then Silhouette Special Edition has everything you've been looking for.

Get 6 books each month before they are available anywhere else!

Act now and we'll send you four exciting Silhouette Special Edition romance novels. They're our gift to introduce you to our convenient home subscription service. Every month, we'll send you six new passion-filled Special Edition books. Look them over for 15 days. If you keep them, pay just $11.70 for all six. Or return them at no charge.

We'll mail your books to you *two full months before they are available* anywhere else. Plus, with every shipment, you'll receive the Silhouette Books Newsletter absolutely free. *And with Silhouette Special Edition there are never any shipping or handling charges.*

Mail the coupon today to get your four free books — and more romance than you ever bargained for.

Silhouette Special Edition is a service mark and a registered trademark of Simon & Schuster, Inc.